THE

HAPPY

CLASS

Russ Morrison's Keys to
Happiness

****

Jay Knight

THE HAPPY CLASS

Russ Morrison's Keys to Happiness

Jay Knight

Charing Cross Press
San Francisco, California

Cataloging-in-Publication data for this book is available from the Library of Congress.

For Sienna, Elisa, Jacob and baby Kater
Suzie the Pug and Q

And for Lisa, Jess, Ronit, Katie,
Cannon, Dan, Danny, Scott,
Mom, Dad, Jane and Glenn

And Taylor, Julian, Virgil, Mark and Andrew

1

This is a story of events that took place six years ago and was written not as a guide to happiness, but just a story. Since this book was first made publicly available, it quickly created an intense following with people using it to make their own lives happier.

If you are simply interested in a summary of the book's lessons, it is available for free as a 20-page booklet "The Happy Class Keys". You can get the booklet at www.the-happy-class.com. You can read it on the site or print it from the PDF that is there.

An additional copy of "The Happy Class Keys" is included at the end of this book to use as a reference to utilize this story to better your life.

2

I am older now. I know that some things in life start out great and turn out terrible and other things start out terrible and turn out great. 2008 was like that to me. It is when I learned these keys to happiness.

+++++++

January 1, 2008 --- My year started out as pretty much of a disaster. On New Year's Day, I broke up with my long-time girlfriend, Rachel. Well... actually, she was more than just a girlfriend, Rachel was my fiancée. And... to be honest, she broke up with me rather than the other way around.

On that New Year's Eve, Rachel and I had been engaged for nine months with only another six months before our scheduled June wedding. We had met while I was in law school, moved in with each other after graduation, and soon starting planning our lives together permanently. Then, at our company's New Year's Eve party, I found out she was having an affair with my boss. Let's just say this discovery was not a good moment for me.

The whole thing was a surreal, zombie-like experience. It was more like something I would read in a novel than an event that was actually happening. The first 48 hours remain a blur. I know I was breathing, and I even ate, but I really do not remember much except going home, packing a suitcase, and ending up at a Marriot hotel six blocks away.

As it turned out, I not only lost my planned future wife that night, I also lost my job. I was working as a second-year lawyer in a large law firm in Chicago. I wasn't fired, but despite a typical lawyer's ability to ignore the facts of a case to advocate for a client, I could not ignore the facts of my fiancé and my boss. One week after finding out these facts, I resigned.

So very quickly, I found myself with no apartment (it was hers), no money (courtesy of no job), and no one to talk to ('my' friends were 'our friends' and I just couldn't figure out how to talk to them about all that had happened). The week after I resigned, I moved back home. I was twenty-seven years old and back living in my mother's house.

I moved back to Racine, Wisconsin, just seventy-five miles north from Chicago. But to me, the two places have little in common. Chicago has career opportunities, happening bars and all sorts of temptations (basically brighter lights and darker alleys). Racine has almost none of either.

Racine has a small town feel even with its 75,000 residents. With only three public high schools, everyone sort of knows everyone else (or at least someone in every family in town).

Still for me, Racine has always been special. It contains my childhood friends and memories of little league games, high school poker nights, and first kisses... all the potential healing ingredients that my newly hired therapist recommended.

Above all, Racine is where my mother still lives. My dad died when I was four. I was an only child and she was a single mom... that situation usually leads to a strong bond, and it did with us.

For the first two weeks home, my mother treated me like a convalescent patient recovering from major surgery. I just watched numbing television while she went to work – as a pediatric nurse at the local hospital. I picked up some books to read, but I could not concentrate enough to enjoy them. Only the mindlessness of television game shows or old reruns seemed to work to dull everything I was feeling.

When this process had stretched to the third and fourth week, the therapy started. My mother handed me a card with three names and phone numbers on it. She said I should pick one. I picked Lois Smith. The other two were men, and I just couldn't picture myself telling another man how low I felt about what had happened.

I knew nothing about therapy except what I had seen in the movies – and I was a bit apprehensive about the first appointment. I was even nervous that a friend might see me going into the therapy office. In the last month, I had seen a couple of old high school friends, but I had confided in no one about what had happened to me in Chicago. So 'explaining' a therapy appointment was not something I wanted to deal with at the moment.

The first session was sort of okay… just Lois asking me about my life. We talked about my growing up in Racine, my friends, my girlfriends, the loss of my father, and even the end of my relationship with Rachel.

Lois was good enough to get me through the break-up as more of a factual history lesson than the 'touchy/feely and angst' stuff I was expecting. I thought she would ask me how I felt about all these things the next time. For the first appointment, she pretty much left me to tell her the 'just what happened'.

For the next few days, I wondered how I would handle everything when she starting asking the tough questions – I was dreading it and frankly tried not to think about it. Of course, the more I tried not to think about what she would ask, the more I imagined the questions and my answers. I even dreamt about her asking, "Jay, what did you really feel?" I would answer as best I could, and she would ask again and again and – then I woke up.

That session with Lois never happened.

A much different course intervened. My next session with Lois was a discussion of an unusual offer I had received.

It was an offer to spend three months in California with my father's uncle (my dad's mother's brother to be exact). A great-uncle I had met only once at my father's funeral when I was just four. A great-uncle my mother rarely mentioned, except if someone asked who all of our relatives were. A great-uncle who called my mother to ask if I might be available to help him out with some legal work for a couple of months. A great-uncle who now gave me an 'out' from 'out of the blue' in more ways than one.

I was not home when he called, so my mother talked to him. He told her what he had in mind, but not really why he had called me and not someone else. I was to call him back with questions the next night. My second therapy session was scheduled that afternoon, so… that is how a strange offer became the only topic of conversation at my second therapy session.

"So what are you going to tell him tonight?" Lois asked it so simply and directly after I had told her about the offer that it jolted me a bit. I guess I had been working at not thinking about actually making a decision.

"Ah… I think I will turn it down. I mean… well, ah… I'm not sure I'm ready right now to leave here. And… ah… I guess I have therapy with you and ah… my mom and…."

"I see," Lois paused for a couple of seconds and then continued. "There is a saying I heard one of my professors offer in a lecture a long time ago – 'Don't let therapy get in the way of real life.' I have always tried to follow his suggestion. I am sure there is at least one good therapist for you to see in California…"

She paused again, then added, "Are you afraid the legal work will be too hard or perhaps too easy?"

"No, it's not that. He told my mother the work was basically dealing with the law firms he's hired to help with some contracts. I think I could do the work just fine. It is more that I have had so much change recently, I'm not sure I need any more."

Lois responded, "Or maybe more change is just what you need. Something new and absorbing so you can get your feet on the ground again... just a thought."

We talked more on how to make the decision, and then she spoke the words used in almost all therapy sessions... 'Our time is up' and I was out the door.

I don't know what made me say "yes". Maybe it was his tone of voice. Maybe it was his disarming words – 'Just call me Russ', which was almost the first thing he said. But mostly, there was something captivating in his words and the passion he had for 'your adventure' as he called his offer to me.

Somehow I said yes before I knew it... I agreed to drive out and be there in a week. After I hung up, I immediately wanted to change what I had said. I wanted to call him back and say I made a mistake. But I didn't. When I told my mother that I had said 'yes', she just smiled and said that she agreed. 'It seems like a good plan for you'. I even thought I saw a bit of a twinkle in her eye as she said it. It was then that she told me 'Uncle Russ' was a bit like my father and that was why she thought it was a good idea. And she left it at that.

The next two days I kept busy getting my car serviced for the long drive and picking out what to take with me.

Packing was easy – I had a whole car to put my stuff in and I really didn't own much more than clothes. 'Uncle Russ' said I would be living in the guest cottage at his home, so I didn't need anything major.

I spent one night out with two friends from high school who were still in Racine and one night out with my mom. She wanted to cook me a home meal, and I wanted to treat her to her favorite, a T-bone steak, to thank her for letting me back in my room for a month. For such a petite woman, my mom can devour a pretty big steak and baked potato dinner. It was a nice evening.

3

The next morning, I was off.

In the passenger seat, I had a basket full of snacks and a cooler full of water and some artificial ice. With my iPod full of music hooked up to the car stereo, I was as ready as I would ever be for what was to come.

I was planning on leaving at seven and getting to somewhere in the middle of Nebraska before I stopped for the night. But Mom's pancakes and goodbyes slowed me down. On the other hand, Racine has no 'rush hour' traffic, so it really made little difference when I left. I waved goodbye to Mom in the driveway and' bye' to Lake Michigan, as I drove away from the house. 'My adventure', as Uncle Russ had called it, had now begun.

I had settled on 'Uncle Russ' for what I would call my father's uncle and my new employer. I decided I was just too young to call him "Russ" as he suggested, and I really didn't know him well enough to use that name. I am not sure why I felt that way, but I just did.

I had driven west about five miles to the highway out of town when it first 'hit' me, and it 'hit' me like a ton of bricks. My life as I had envisioned it ever since I was fifteen was over. I knew my life was not over. But my carefully arranged 'plan' was over. Until the last 60 days, most everything in my life had gone 'according to plan'.

My plan had been simple. Go to school, study, play basketball, meet girls, go to college, study harder, meet more girls, go to law school, studier even harder, meet my future wife, move to the big city, get great job, get engaged, get married…. or not. Then there came the reality – lose girl, quit job, move back home, be unemployed, be unmotivated, be a loser.

A loud honking sound broke my thoughts. The stoplight I was waiting for had turned green. I quickly stepped on the accelerator. A bit too fast, and my tires squealed as I shot forward. I felt even more embarrassed.

That scenario was pretty much my whole trip. I tried to listen to my IPod, but constantly my thoughts came back to how much loss I had suffered since New Year's Eve. I was pretty sure that for the rest of my life I would hate that celebration….

Of course, there was one obvious question I had not figured out an answer to yet.

Why did Uncle Russ make his offer to me? And why now?

I had wanted to ask Russ, but the right moment never came up in our call. I tried to ask my Mom, but she just dodged the question with a 'How would I know?' type answer. It was mysterious and a bit discomforting to me. I figured I would find out when I got to California, and if I did not like the answer I could always just turn around drive back to Racine. Despite my positive attitude to that question, it still came back to me every few hours.

As I drove, I realized I was in no mood to 'see the country'. So, I got on Interstate 80 and drove straight west. Basically the drive was flat, then the drive was mountains, then flat, then mountains and then on the fourth day, I was there, crossing the Bay Bridge from Oakland into San Francisco.

As it turned out, Uncle Russ lived just south of San Francisco in the hills above what is known as Silicon Valley. Uncle Russ later told me that he originally bought his farm on the foggy side of the mountain ridge as a weekend retreat when he was in his early thirties. That was when land in the San Francisco area was still affordable. After his kids went to college, he moved to his 'Farm' full time.

I pulled up to the Farm's gate a little before six in the evening. The sun was close to setting, but I could still see everything really well. Just before getting to the driveway into the Farm, in the far distance, I saw the Pacific Ocean between the trees with the sun gleaming on the water.

The gate was solid wood, simple but sturdy. It was the kind of gate that swings open with a motor when someone 'buzzes you in'. There was a fairly high wooden fence running along the road on both sides of the gate. With bushes and trees on both sides of the fence, it was ascetically pleasing, yet very private at the same time.

The gate itself was indented off the road, so I turned off and stopped my car in front of it. I looked around for how to get in. I then noticed one of those typical code panel boxes on a pole a few feet to my left. Rather than back up and try to pull closer, I decided to just open the car door, get out, and walk over. I had been driving for days and stretching even briefly felt good.

Along with the keypad, there was a big green button with a note above it saying 'Press to talk'. So I did. I heard quick telephone dialing tones and then some ringing. After about five rings, a woman answered the phone.

"Hello?"

I leaned over to the box. "Hi, this is Jay Knight. Ah...
I'm here at the gate." One second after I said that, I thought.
*Duh, of course she knows I am at the gate, how else could I
have rung the buzzer?*

Thankfully, she ignored my stupidity.

"I'll open the gate. Just take the paved road all the
way up to the front of the house, and someone will meet you
there."

The gate was already starting to open, so I quickly
said, "Okay. Thanks." I got back in my car and hurried to get
my seatbelt fastened so the gate would not close back. I had
no idea how long it would stay open.

As it turned out, the gate swung very wide, and I had
plenty of time to drive through. On the other side, the paved
road went straight, and about 50 feet ahead, two dirt/hard
packed gravel roads headed off in opposite directions,
creating an intersection. I could see a couple of muddy tire
tracks that other vehicles had made coming off the dirt roads
and turning onto the paved one.

I was starting to get a bit nervous. I really did not
know what to expect of the next couple of months, but now I
was certainly about to find out. Ready or not.

Once past the intersection, two things occurred, the
road curved to the right and headed down a small hill. It

headed into a short stretch of giant redwood trees, towering to me what looked like 100 feet or more. Past that spot, the road continued further down a bit and the landscape opened up with some big oak trees and then the house.

I do not know what I was expecting, but it wasn't this view. The driveway went toward the right side of the house and then in front of the house, it made a complete circle.

The house was long, single story in the front and quite modern. From the front door in the middle of the house, the right side had a wing that headed away at an angle and continued about 80 to 100 feet. The land dropped away, and at some point the house became two stories with an additional story appearing underneath. To the left of the front door, the house continued even farther than on the right, probably another 120 to 150 feet when again the land dropped away and at the far end of the left wing another level appeared under the first.

After looking left and right, I got the impression that probably the whole hill dropped away behind the house, and thus on the backside, the whole house was probably two stories. The modern style was a bit reminiscent of the Frank Lloyd Wright houses I had seen growing up in Wisconsin. It had the flair and dramatic look of his flowing indoor-outdoor wood beams.

The entry was large, and the door looked at least twelve feet tall. The door was open, and a woman was standing in front of it. I pulled to a stop, and she walked behind the car to greet me. I opened my door and pulled myself out of the car.

She put out her hand, as I stood up. I shook it as she said. "Hi Jay. I'm Diana, Russ's assistant. He apologizes for not greeting you after your long drive. A long call just came in and he asked if I could show you around and get you settled."

"That would be great. Thanks. Should I get a bag?"

"No, you are staying in one of cottages on the other side of the house. You can just drive your car up to it. It will be much easier."

"Okay. Great." I followed her toward the front door. She was tall, at least 5' 10". As I am 6 feet tall, she pretty much looked at me eye to eye. She was thin, in a sporty sort of way, with long brown hair, wearing jeans and a white, men's style button-up shirt. I guessed she was about my age, twenty–six or twenty-seven.

As we walked in, I was blown away. I had been right. The house was two stories all along the back with an additional level below the one we had entered. We walked about twenty feet into the house to a railing. Beyond the railing, the floor below appeared, and the room grew to twenty foot ceilings with floor-to-ceiling windows. The view out the windows was the one I had seen from the road, only better. The hills rolled down, and while the ocean was still six to seven miles away, you had an unobstructed view of nearly twenty miles of coastline.

The room below expanded in both directions with a wall of windows fifty to sixty feet long. We stood on a balcony, and the room seemed to continue under us, which I later found out was true. To the right was a pool table, a fireplace with a very large flat screen TV above it and chairs and sofas in a half circle around it. To the left, was a large simple, wooden dining table and then further left a very large kitchen with an eating counter and hoods and stuff. The whole area was open to twenty feet high and decorated in a simple and inviting manner.

I hadn't moved or said a word yet. Then I heard Diana's voice.

"Yeah... Pretty special the first time you see this view. I have learned to let most new visitors take a second before moving on."

"Thanks," I said. "This may be the most spectacular room I have ever been in."

"Me too. One of the perks of working here. Although you need to know that fog causes a sunset view like this one today to be less than common." She motioned me toward the hallway to the right. We walked a few steps.

"Down this hallway are a couple of offices. There's mine, one I set up for you, and then Russ's. Past his office is Russ's bedroom which, like this room, is two stories, but in a different way."

We did not go that way. Instead, Diana spun us around, and we headed the other way past the big room and toward the much bigger wing. As we passed the big room, Diana, turned and said. "By the way, everyone calls this room 'the kitchen'. So if someone says 'they will meet you in the kitchen', they mean somewhere down there."

We continued down the hallway with Diana pointing out what must have been 6 or 7 bedrooms which she described as the family guest rooms. They were most often used by Russ's children or grandchildren.

At this point, I had been with Diana for about 15 minutes or so and I was trying to figure out more about her. But I had no clue. She was obviously totally at ease in the house, and at the same time, it was obvious she was not part of the family. She was professional and yet warm and friendly.

We reached the end of the hall and Diana swung open the double doors. We stepped onto a small balcony that overlooked a very large room below.

"The game room." She waved her arm as a way of showing grandeur. Although with the big smile on her face, I knew it was mock grandeur. "It really is quite the room." She continued, as we stood there peering down.

I tried hard to gather it all in. It was spread out sort of everywhere. There was a ping pong table, foosball, and air hockey, three of my teenage favorites. Then as I looked more, there was also a large basketball area and along the far wall two full-sized bowling lanes fully equipped just like a real bowling alley. This array was in addition to tables for games, drawing, a crafts area, and plenty of just run-around room for little kid stuff. A few of arcade- sized video games gave the whole room the feel of a kid's fantasyland.

"Come on. Let's go down this way. We can head back to the kitchen and check in with Anna."

Anna…? I wondered who Anna was?

As we came down to the floor level, I realized how cool this room really was. I followed Diana through a path to a wide hallway leading out of the room.

While you were down among all the games and other stuff, the room seemed to want you to turn one on and play.

"I'll bet Russ's kids loved this room," I said.

Diana stopped and said, "As I understand it, this room was added after Katlin went off to college, so they never really lived with it. I have been told that the real kid in the family is Russ. As far as I can tell that is very true."

The hallway we headed down was on the outside, so on one side there were large windows still letting in light from the now almost set sun. We stopped. Diana opened a door to another room and quickly turned on the lights.

"This is the theatre. We live so far from a movie theatre that this is a great place to see movies."

I looked in. There were five rows of extra-large plush movie seats. The floor sloped down quite a bit with a nice large screen at the other end. On one side, I saw a small soda fountain and a movie theater style popcorn popper.

"Very cool," I said. I had about run out of words after the game room. "Must be hard to figure out what to do first here."

"I think you will find that most of this stuff is used quite a bit. Russ has eight grandchildren and most nights here are too cold and foggy to be outside. I think he built all this, so they would want to visit him often. We are pretty remote, but this and the farm work well... Let's head to the kitchen. But just so you know, the laundry and storage and supply rooms are on the other side of the kitchen directly underneath the offices we first saw."

"Great. I'm sure I will be able to find them when I need to."

We walked into the kitchen section of 'the kitchen' and there was a woman whom I presumed was Anna stirring a couple of pots on the stove. "Spaghetti at seven." The woman said without turning around.

"Anna, it's me. Diana. I really wanted to introduce you to Jay."

Anna turned around quickly looking a bit the embarrassed. "Oh. Sorry. I thought you were one of kids. Nine times out of ten all they want is 'what and when'..." She wiped her right hand on a towel and reached out to me.

"Jay was it? I'm Anna. Nice to meet you."

I shook her hand. "Nice to meet you Anna. Smells wonderful." I wasn't just making that up either. I was either starving, or this was going to be a great spaghetti dinner... or both.

"Why thank you, I hope you will be staying."

Diana answered before I could. "Yes Jay will be here for dinner. Actually, he will be helping Russ over the next couple of months. He is staying in Cottage Six."

Anna looked back at me. "Welcome to Casa Russ." Then she turned to stir the spaghetti sauce some more.

Diana motioned for me to follow her. "I'm taking Jay out to his cottage now. He needs time to unpack."

We headed out of the cooking area of the kitchen, past the big dining table, and to a set of stairs under the balcony from where I had first viewed this giant space. As we climbed the stairs, Diana said, "By the way, Russ does not care if you are late for dinner, but Anna does. So..."

And then we both said the words at the same time, "Best not be late." Diana stopped and smiled at me and gave me a quick 'thumbs up'.

Once out the front door and next to my car, Diana pointed to a small branch off the main driveway that went past the house on the left- hand side.

"Take this little path. Just past the house, the cottages will start on the left. You are in number 6. Can't miss it. There is a big lighted 6 on the door. Just park your car next to the cottage. The door is unlocked, and the keys are inside."

She paused, so I reassured her. "I think I can do that. Sounds easy."

"It is... You have almost an hour before dinner which should be plenty of time to unpack while it is still light out. When you are ready, there is a small lighted footpath that will take you from the cottages right to the kitchen. I'll see you there."

"Thanks." And with that I got in my car and started it.

The cottages began right after the road curved past the main house, and very quickly I was at number six. I pulled up in a little parking space next to it and got out to look at what would be new home for the next three months. Since the road had been heading downhill quite a bit, the hill behind the cottages was rising. I saw there were lots of redwood trees on the hill just behind the cottage.

All the cottages looked pretty much alike even if they were different shapes. They were built mainly of big stones with wood-framed windows. All of them had little porches across the front and a fairly steep roof made of what looked like slate.

I grabbed my small cooler from the passenger seat, carried it to the front door and let myself in. It was a bit darker than I was expecting, but then the sunlight was really starting to fade. I flipped the lights on to find a nice small living area with an open counter to the kitchen behind. I set my cooler on the counter and walked over to the bedroom.

I turned the light on and found a simple, but big room with a large bed and what looked like a big closet. Last was the bathroom. Another nice surprise, the bathroom was big with a spa tub and a walk- in shower. I was starting to think that my 'adventure' at my Uncle Russ's may have been a really wise decision.

When I had first heard that I was 'banished' to the cottages from the main house, I was a bit disappointed. I now saw it was a bonus given to me. The privacy offered here and the niceness of the space made it a much better place for me than the main house.

I went back to the car and in three more trips, I had all my bags and boxes in the living room. In no time, I had it all put away. I noticed a few supplies in the kitchen including snacks like microwave popcorn, chips and soda. I guessed these cottages were often used by visitors to the Farm… I found out later that it was a good guess.

I took a quick shower, put on a clean shirt and my jeans, and got ready to head back up to the main house. I found myself humming an old tune as I finished up.

I'm humming. I must be feeling better about coming out here. I remember thinking at the time.

The nervousness from my first arrival had given way to more of an excitement in the moment. I had only met Diana and Anna, and yet I already liked being here. *Interesting…*

Then that 'mystery' question returned. It was the one that had kept popping into my brain on the drive out. '*Why me? Why now?" Maybe I will find out at dinner… maybe not…*

4

When I opened the cottage door, I immediately noticed it was both darker and colder than just an hour before. I thought about getting a jacket, but the house was so close that it seemed silly. There were small lights on the car path next to the cottages, and at cottage number three, a lighted footpath led up the hill to the main house. The hill blocked a view of the house from my cottage, and as I walked up the path, the house seemed to just appear over the top of it. Soon I was on the patio outside 'the kitchen'.

As I approached one of the doors, I could see Diana, Anna and Uncle Russ inside. I recognized him from a photo I had looked up on the Internet. In addition, there were three kids whom I found out later were nine to fourteen. They were more or less in the cooking section of the room with Anna going back and forth in what looked like last minute moves to prepare dinner.

I opened the door.

"There he is." Russ walked over to greet me. "Jay, so good to meet you in person." He looked straight into my eyes as he shook my hand. "I hope you brought your hunger from

Wisconsin. Anna makes a very special spaghetti meat sauce. And she almost expects everyone to have seconds."

He was taller than I expected, at least one or two inches taller than me. He wore blue jeans and a nice casual button-down shirt.

"Nice to meet you too. I'm pretty hungry after the drive. So I think I can hold my own."

"That is great. Now, I know you've already met Diana and Anna. So let me introduce three of my grandchildren." They had already gathered around us, boy, girl, boy… oldest first.

"Jay, this is Alex. Plays a mean game of air hockey."

Alex put out his hand to shake mine. "Nice to meet you."

Russ continued quickly with, "This is Alicia who I think holds the record for the most text messages sent in an hour." I shook her hand, as she rolled her eyes at her grandfather. You could tell there was that 'special communication' between the two of them by the way a smile sneaked across her face.

"Nice to meet you, Jay. GP told us you will be spending a couple of months here."

"I think that is the plan." I responded wondering to myself who GP was, but I figured I would find out later.

Russ then introduced the last of his group. "And this is Kevin. I will let Kevin speak for himself, he usually does."

Kevin stepped closer and put out his hand. "Is it true that you are a lawyer?"

I smiled and shook his hand. "Yes Kevin I am a lawyer. Why do you ask?"

"I'm having an argument with my sister, and I was thinking that I might need to hire someone to help me win. I thought that if GP hired you then you must be good. And so, I was wondering what your rates might be."

Russ stepped in with a smile. "All good thoughts, Kevin, but let's have dinner first, and then you can work on figuring out your 'domestic disputes' with your sister. However, I will go on record that my hiring Jay does not preclude him from working on other matters that any of you may want to bring to him. Now let's eat before Anna tells us it's too cold."

The kids quickly formed a line next to a small pile of plates on one of the countertops. I found myself next to Diana. She leaned in and said. "This is the standard meal service here, buffet style. Seems to work well. If someone is late, they simply get their own food, and if Anna wants to serve certain portions of anything, she can control portion size if she wants to."

The kids quickly loaded their plates with whatever they wanted. I noticed there was no talk of what to eat or not to eat… I learned more about that part later.

Russ spoke when Alex, who was first, was just sitting down at the table.

"Please leave a place next to me for Jay at this first meal. I have not had a chance to greet him yet and would like to be able to say a few words at dinner. Thank you."

I noticed Alex adjust his plate one seat over from where he had first headed apparently indicating a place for me.

When I took my plate and got a closer look at the food, I was struck at how orderly it had been set out. Anna obviously counted 'presentation' as one of her cooking responsibilities. It all looked great and smelled great. I was going to have to show some self-discipline not to pile too much food on my plate.

A salad, pasta, meat sauce, meatballs were just the start. There were vegetables, breads and a half-dozen other things as well. I took it easy on quantity (I had already been told seconds were possible) and then went over to the table to sit down. There were two empty places between Alex and Alicia, so I sat in the one next to Alex. I noticed everyone was waiting to eat until the last person was seated. My mind was spinning, full of a lot of new information.

So GP is Russ, must be short for grandpa... the kids are very well behaved despite what seems as no instruction... and why are the grandchildren here at all?... where are the parents??? It seems so normal. Maybe this is always how it is?

Russ and Anna came to the table at almost the same time with Russ sitting next to me at one end of the table and Anna taking an empty chair next to Diana. While there were seven of us, the table had ten chairs, leaving three empty ones. I later learned the table was built, so one could add several large leaves and it could accommodate 20+ diners, if needed.

As soon as Anna sat, the kids began to eat. I guess politeness went just so far. Anna reached for a bottle of wine she had placed on the table earlier and asked, "Jay or Diana, I am going to have a glass of Chianti with my spaghetti. Do either of you want one?

Diana, now in the middle of chewing, raised her hand, and I simply said, "That would be great. Thanks." I noticed that not only had Uncle Russ not been offered any wine, but in addition he had a wine glass at his place into which he had poured Diet Coke from a can.

It was just then that Uncle Russ raised his wine glass and said. "I would like us to give a toast of welcome to Jay. I hope his stay here is as pleasant as it is productive."

All of the diners reached for their glasses of either wine, water or whatever they were having. There were some nods, a couple of welcomes and a big smile from Diana, as they all clinked glasses. Alex handed me my glass, so he could clink it and said it was okay for the guest to toast himself. I was thinking that even though I hadn't been here very long, they were doing a fine job of making me feel welcome.

I no sooner finished putting my glass down and was starting to take my first bite of spaghetti when Kevin spoke up.

"I have my Word."

Diana later explained to me that at every dinner with the grandchildren, a family 'game' was played. They called the game 'Word'. Basically, starting from youngest to oldest, a person could pose a word, phrase, or question to be discussed. Uncle Russ was required to give his first thoughts about the word or question, and then, others could add more or not as they saw fit. No one was required to pose a word and could skip their turn. The next dinner they would start with the person that had been next the night before. If they could not remember whose turn it was, it always reverted back to the youngest.

Russ responded, "Okay Kevin. I think it's your turn, so what is the word?"

"Tomorrow, I need to turn in my Little League application if I want to play spring baseball again this year. I want to know how to go about making the decision."

I had heard Kevin try to hire me as his lawyer just 15 minutes earlier, so I was not totally surprised by the complexity of his question. He did not want advice on what to do, just advice on how he could figure out what to do by himself. Pretty cool for a nine-year old.

"Ah... baseball." Russ almost sighed. "I need to confess that baseball is my least favorite sport. I was so afraid of being hit by a pitch I never swung at anything. Mainly, I was always getting ready to jump out of the way. My best friend was our best pitcher, and one day the coach came up with a plan to help me get rid of my fear. He had me stand at the plate and have my friend pitch to me until I hit one. He knelt behind me and with hands on my waist, he held me firmly, so I could not jump away.

The result was disastrous. My friend hit me four times, and I never hit even one pitch. After that, I dreaded every baseball game and every softball game I ever played."

"So Kevin, you've been thinking about this. What do you think are the important factors for you making a decision about you and Little League? If anyone sees what they think is a 'killer app', speak up."

Killer app?

Diana later explained that Russ taught a simple way to make decisions and one element was what he called a 'killer app'. That is when one factor outweighed everything else and made a decision easy, unless of course there was a 'killer app' on the other side. "Killer app' was a term borrowed from software developers who were always looking for the one use of their software that overrode all the objections to it.

Kevin again spoke like a little scientist. "Things I think are important are that many of my friends play Little League and I suck at baseball."

"Those are two pretty good reasons not to know what to do. I would guess it would be good to follow the results of both sides of the decision. Okay?"

"Okay."

I looked around the table to find everyone eating, but also paying attention to the discussion.

"Let's look at the 'I suck and want to quit' side first. Kevin, I don't suppose you feel you are going to get good at baseball no matter how much you try – you sound too much like your grandfather."

"I strike out almost every time I come to bat. I can throw the ball pretty well. But I can't catch it. I do not like it when kids on the other team yell 'easy out' when it's my turn to hit."

"But you like being on the team with all your friends. Correct?"

"Yes."

"Well, you already know what it's like to be on the team. Can you imagine what it's like not to be in Little League?"

"What do you mean?"

"What would you do, and how would you feel? Would you just sit around your room feeling sorry for yourself, or would do something different. Have you thought about what you would do?"

"Yes, and I have two ideas. One is sign up for spring soccer. Not too many of my friends play, but I'm much better at soccer. Or I could finish the Mr. Science series of projects."

"They both sound good. Which one do you think you would pick?"

"Probably soccer, I know that at least my friend Markus will be there and I think that is better than no one."

"So you can imagine what playing spring soccer would be like?"

"Yeah."

"Okay. So it's time to make your decision. You already know what another year with baseball and your friends will be like. Now imagine being out of baseball and into soccer instead. Which feels best?"

"Soccer....." Kevin was smiling at GP.

About two seconds later, Kevin added, "But GP, I know my mom and dad want me to play baseball. What about them?"

So they are alive.

"Well, Kevin, your life is about you, not anyone else. If you're not happy with what you're doing, you will not be good at making other people happy. No one else gets hurt by your decision, so I think this choice is your decision. Anyway, since I'm supposed to be 'in charge' right now, I will 'take the heat' if there is any. But I can almost guarantee you, they will both agree when you tell them why."

Russ continued, "When your mom was growing up, any decision I made I needed to back up with understandable reasons why I made it and why it was a good decision. If your mom had reasons why she was right, and her reasons were as good as mine or better, then she would win, and we would do things her way."

"Got it," Kevin answered.

I learned later that the words 'got it' were a special shorthand for 'I understand what you are saying, and I will follow it.' Somehow it had permeated the vocabulary at 'the Farm' and everyone used it. 'Got it' also meant it was okay to move on to a new topic.

The new topic turned out to be thanking Anna for preparing the dinner as everyone made a comment about something they liked about it. Diana then announced she would be leaving after lunch the next day to head into San Francisco and then to Napa Valley for the weekend.

"Bummer," Alicia said. "I was hoping you would go riding with me on Saturday. I wanted to try out Bronco on the new course to see if I'm good enough to stay with him."

"I will be here next weekend," Diana replied.

Alicia then turned to me and asked, "Uncle Jay?"

Where did the uncle part come from?

I learned Alicia was excellent at getting her way, and she had calculated if she played 'little girl", I might be more susceptible to saying yes… her plan was about to work.

"Do you know how to ride a horse?"

"A little bit."

"Would you ride a little with me on Saturday?" Before I could answer, Russ stepped in with his comment.

"Jay, just because Alicia is manipulative enough to ask you on your first night here, you needn't say 'yes' unless you want to go riding."

Does he want me to say no, or is he just being a good host?

Since I had learned to ride a bit on a Wisconsin farm that one of my high school buddies lived on, I decided to say 'yes'. "Alicia, I'd enjoy riding with you as long as you understand it has been at least ten years since I have ridden a horse, and I was not that great back then."

"Done." – I learned this was the twin of 'got it.' It meant a deal was struck and all conditions accepted. I would learn a whole new language from Russ's grandkids over the next months.

Alicia continued, "We can meet here in the kitchen at ten on Saturday morning. Okay?"

"Got it," I answered. I was trying to learn quickly. Alicia smiled in return.

Alex addressed his grandfather, "GP, may I be excused? I have a math test tomorrow, and I want to review tonight."

"Sure. Anyone wanting some fruit and ice cream, Anna says there are lots of different berries in the refrigerator. If anyone wants to join me, I'm having mine next to the fireplace." Then turning to me he said, "Jay, if you are not too tired, I would be happy if you'd join me."

"Ah… sure," I responded, not knowing if I 'really' had a choice or not at this point.

Diana announced she had some work to finish because of her short day tomorrow. She gave me a smile and a wave and left. Kevin also scooted off to his room. Alicia stayed to help clean the dishes. It turned out this job rotated daily and even Russ had an evening when he was the helper.

I followed Russ into the work area of the kitchen where the oversized freezer and refrigerator were located. There were a few bowls stacked with spoons, previous planned preparation by Anna it appeared.

Peering into the refrigerator, Russ asked, "We have blueberries, strawberries, raspberries and blackberries. And there are some bananas on the counter if you would prefer them."

"Strawberries and raspberries sound good. Thanks."

Russ put those two and some blueberries on the counter. -- "I'm not sure what flavors of ice cream we have, but can you get the vanilla bean for me? I know we always have that."

I opened the giant freezer door and saw there were a few containers of vanilla bean. I grabbed one that looked like it had already been opened and put it on the counter next to the berries. Then I saw a carton of Dutch Chocolate – I'm a sucker for Dutch Chocolate so I took out that too.

Russ and I built small piles of ice cream and berries in our bowls. I followed him over to the other side of 'the kitchen', where a half dozen soft chairs and a loveseat made a semi-circle around the fireplace. It was not the old-fashioned fireplace with logs burning, but rather an excellent replica fed by natural gas and a glass front with heat coming out the surrounding vents. I was surprised to hear the cracking pops usually only heard with wood burning.

When we sat, Russ offered, "Used to have a log fireplace, but in the remodel I lost it to new building codes given the amount of windows in this room. Actually, this is pretty good, and no clean-up the next day is a big plus."

I nodded. "I'm surprised at the amount of heat it puts out. Makes it nice and cozy." I took a big bite of my ice cream and berries.

"Yes, I do enjoy sitting here reading a good book. But the reason I wanted you to join me was to ask what questions you might have and explain a bit about what will happen the next couple of days."

He continued, "I assume the cottage is fine?"

"Oh yes. It's perfect."

"Well, the cottages were on the property when I bought it forty-years ago. I do not know why they were built. My best guess is that the original owner rented them out in the summer as vacation rentals to make extra money."

"When I moved here as my primary residence, I did a lot to make this a place where I could get my family and friends to stay for weekends or whatever. So I had eight of them turned into private little cottages. That way my guests would not feel like they were living in someone else's house."

"It works," I added. Russ took a small spoonful of ice cream and berries.

"Well, it has been better than expected. Right now Diana lives in #1 during the week and she spends many weekends in San Francisco. Anna moved into #2 about ten or twelve years ago after her son went off to college. It's a bit larger with two bedrooms so when he comes to visit, he has his own room."

I found I was still a bit nervous around Russ even with his low key approach to everything. No questions had

43

popped into my mind yet. After a brief silence Russ saved me from asking something stupid.

"So tomorrow is your first official day. You can start whenever you want. Diana usually starts at about 8:30, but again you pick your own time."

"I have a long early call tomorrow morning with my Paris partners and right afterwards, I have to go into Palo Alto. In the afternoon, I will be up in San Francisco picking up my other daughter's twins. They're coming here for the weekend. We should be back in time for dinner."

Russ paused for another bite of ice cream. I already had a mouthful so we both just ate in silence for a few seconds. Then he continued.

"I only tell you this schedule, as it's your first day and I would have preferred to be here for you. That said, Diana has arranged some files and charts. They will give you a summary of all of my business affairs. Don't be afraid to ask Diana any questions. We have a 'no secrets' policy here – I have found that no secrets' reduces bad surprises which are always hard to handle."

"Anyway, you and I can sit down Monday morning, and I will go through in detail all the help I need…. How does that sound?"

"Sounds good." My mind now understood the plan as he laid it out.

"Good. Let me give you a quick introduction to the Farm and answer any of the questions that I'm sure you have."

No pressure, but this is the second time he has asked for questions. Surely I can think of at least one good one...

"I bought the original property almost 40 years ago. I had just sold a business that I'd started with a friend and the real estate market was in one of its periodic dips. The old guy who built this house had died, and his heirs just wanted to cash out."

"Over the years, I tried to buy anything else that was next to or near the original property. It gives the Farm a somewhat irregular shape. I haven't bought anything in a few years though. I think the local realtors figured out I was a sucker and they could overprice the neighboring properties. So I stopped buying. Then later, California land prices became too high for a simple farm."

"The house here is pretty high on the property, and most of the Farm runs down the hills towards the ocean. I do have one nice parcel up higher. The kids like to go riding up there as it is the least foggy."

Russ had put down his bowl and was using his hands to sort of point in the direction of the land he was talking about.

"At the bottom of the property, I have three joint ventures. One is the stables where Alicia will take you on Saturday. We board lots of horses there, and I have a few of my own. Quite honestly, it is a breakeven operation, but it allows me to entice the grandkids with the horses that they all seem to love."

"The other two ventures are in agriculture. One is an artichoke farm, and the larger one a cut flower operation. They both do quite well. You'll see that in the books tomorrow."

"Off and on over the years I've tried cattle and sheep ranching, both were more work than they were worth. So I gave them up."

"For many years, this was only an occasional weekend retreat. I was living in Palo Alto, and it was a great way to escape the urban life and yet only be 30 minutes away. After my youngest, Katlin, started college, I started coming here more and not going back to Palo Alto. Eventually, I sold the house there and moved here full time."

"You'll see, it's often foggy here. But we are high enough up on the mountain, so many days we are above the fog for much of the day while the coast itself is completely socked in."

I looked out the window and with some of the outdoor lighting, you could see fog right up on the patio.

"I love the tranquility and the nature and even though I'm not much of a farmer, I have learned a bit more. I am fascinated by all the improvements in the healthy ways to grow food."

"But mainly, I rebuilt the place to attract the grandkids. It has worked. I love having them around. They are the real joy of my life right now."

Russ paused a bit and took a spoonful of ice cream, now melting a little.

At this point, one good question did pop into my brain.

"I was wondering about Alex, Alicia and Kevin. They seem very at ease here. If I'm not prying, why are they living with you?"

"Good question," Russ answered quickly. "Their parents, my daughter Katlin and her husband, agreed to do a project with the World Bank which involves travel and changing locations about every two weeks. That was too stressful to drag the kids with them. So they asked if they could stay with me."

"It started in January and was supposed to end in April, but it looks now like it might be sometime in June before their parents get back."

"It's not too hard. Luckily, they normally live nearby in Portola Valley, so to get them to school takes only about 30 minutes. And I'm of course in heaven with them here…"

We chatted a bit about his children and grandchildren. The youngest was Katlin and her husband, who were both economics professors at Stanford, and their three kids, Alex, Alicia and Kevin. The next oldest was Monique. Monique was divorced, and now a partner in a small, but successful, art gallery. She lived in San Francisco with her twin 16 year-old daughters, Estelle and Charlotte. The oldest, Mark, was married, worked for Google, lived in Los Gatos and had three children Marci 12, Loren 15 and Dan 18.

While we were talking about the kids, I brought up how he had helped Kevin figure out his Little League decision. I told him how I liked the logical approach.

"Well, decision-making is one of the hardest things for many people, especially personal decisions. They fret about it, procrastinate about it, and in the end feel frustrated and nervous even after they've made a decision."

He continued on. "By definition, most personal decisions are about changing something, like moving to a new location or changing jobs. Just as obvious is that if a person is thinking about a change, then they are probably unhappy about some part of their current situation."

"I call my method of making these kinds of decisions 'the box'. Just picture yourself in a box with high walls on all sides, but open at the top. The box is your current situation. Now figure out all the 'costs' of getting out of the box. There are always 'costs', like having to give up friends, or job security, or the good things about your current location. Take your time thinking about these costs, and get them all in the box."

"Then imagine yourself out of the box. What will it feel like? What will you be doing? No 'rose-colored glasses'; just do a realistic assessment."

"Now compare the costs of being out of the box. Is there an obvious winner? If the winner is 'change', make the change. But just as important is that if the winner is 'no change', then stop thinking about it. You have examined the choices and are making the right decision. Of course, later, new facts may arise and change the equation, but then, you can do the process again."

I was impressed how he just 'rolled out' a simple-to-follow process for making important personal decisions. Like my decision to come here. *I wonder if I would have come out here if I had used 'the box'...*

Just as I was pondering that question, Alicia and Kevin showed up in their pajamas.

"Do we get story time?" Alicia asked.

"Ah…" Russ paused for a second. "Yes, of course. Ask your brother if he wants to join us." They ran upstairs yelling for Alex

Russ turned to me. "Most nights we have a short story time before they go to bed. You're welcome to stay or head back to your cottage if you want to."

Before I could react, Alicia and Kevin came running back down the stairs yelling. "He said he's too busy." They jumped onto the love seat facing GP.

I sat down. "Guess I'll stay."

The story process was one they must have done a hundred times. Russ asked them what kind of story they wanted. – Alicia begged Kevin to let it be romance.

Then Russ asked where the story should take place. Kevin said Half Moon Bay – Alicia wanted Paris, but gave in quickly. This back and forth continued for a couple more minutes while picking character names, ages etc.

Then Russ just launched into the story. "It was still light out when Bruce took his last wave in for the day…"

Russ just made up the story as he talked. He occasionally asked the kids which 'direction' the characters might decide to go. Kevin and Alicia were totally captivated and involved.

In twenty minutes, Russ had hit an end point. They both climbed on his lap to give him a hug good night and then went up to their rooms.

We talked some more about family, with Russ asking questions about my mother. At some point, it was time to go to bed. Russ said breakfast during the week was pretty much individual effort although on occasion Anna was known to make scrambled eggs or pancakes and leave them out for people to heat in the microwave.

As I headed to the door, Russ said, "Jay, do you see all the jackets hanging on the coat rack by the door?"

"Yes."

"Take one. They are kept there for people in the cottages. It gets pretty cold here at night."

"Okay I will." I grabbed a jacket and walked out... into the fog, now thicker and wetter than before.

Thank goodness the path to the cottage was well lit. I would have lost my way without it. I noticed I had forgotten to leave any lights on in my cottage, but the bright #6 on the door made it still easy to find.

Once inside, I put the jacket on the coat rack by my door. It already had a jacket hanging on it, which I had missed seeing on my way out.

My mind was still racing a bit.

Wow... six hours... I have been here less than six hours, and already this is a totally different life than I have felt before.

My eye caught the writing journal Lois had told me to buy after our first therapy session. She said it was sometimes good to write things out at the end of a day. I had brought it with me, but so far I hadn't written a word in it.

It was then I decided I wanted to write down Russ's decision box before I forgot it. It was fun to try to remember it just the way he had described it.

I was also thinking that the whole evening had been... *wonderful.* It was the only word that came to my brain. I had thought that this whole experience would be mostly legal advice and some weekend sightseeing. But 'my adventure', as Russ called it, seemed to be about much more than work. One dinner and I was already hooked... and also a bit confused.

What is really going on here?... And why did Russ pick me for this job? I had no better answer now than before I had left Racine.

After I finished writing in my journal, I got out of my clothes, put on a t-shirt and boxers and climbed into bed. There was a nice comforter to use if I was feeling cold. I decided to use it.

Then, out of blue, came a thought – *this is exactly the kind of place Rachel would love. Foggy, mysterious, full of nature… she would wrap her arms around me and demand we make passionate love right now…but that won't happen, not now, not ever…*

My eyes began to tear up. I felt the loss one more time. I was lucky I was so tired from the four days of driving. I fell right to sleep.

5

I woke up to sunlight sneaking around the edge of the drapes and through my bedroom window. For a second, I was confused as to where I was. Then I remembered. Uncle Russ's farm. After that, I remembered I was no longer with Rachel and a small ping of pain hit me. Less than a week ago...I had been in Wisconsin in despair.

Then, I looked at the clock radio next to my bed.

9:30... Shit... I'm already an hour late for Diana...

I jumped out of bed and in 15 minutes I showered, shaved, dressed and was heading up the path to the main house.

The kitchen was empty. There was a bowl of fruit on the dining table. I grabbed a banana and moved directly up the stairs. I headed down the 'office wing' and heard Diana's voice coming from what I assumed was her office.

Should I wait in the hall until she hangs up or go to the doorway so she knows I'm here? ... Finally, I thought... *I'm sure she is wondering what is taking me so long. I guess I will just stick my head in the doorway and see what happens...*

So I stuck my head in the doorway and saw Diana on her phone and looking at her laptop screen as she talked. Her peripheral vision caught my movement, for she looked up in my direction. I gave what must have looked like a silly wave.

She motioned me to a chair next to her desk and held up one finger which I assumed was the universal signal for 'I will just be a minute, please wait.'

I sat down while she continued her call and looked around. It was a small office, just room for her desk, a credenza, and a couple of chairs in front of the desk, one of which I was in. I looked for knickknacks or photos that might tell me a bit more about Diana – there were none. Except there was one photo on the desk facing Diana, so I could not see it. The windows in her room were up high on the wall behind her, so all you could see were the big oak trees that were in the front of the house.

She hung up in a couple of minutes. Before I could speak, she apologized, "Sorry about that... Good morning. I take it you slept well."

"Longer than I thought I would. Sorry I'm so late."

"It's fine." She got up. "Let me show you your office. I put all the materials in there." We went to the office right next to Diana's – it was nearly identical. Just less clutter. Two tall piles of files were stacked on the desk.

"This is yours." Diana motioned me inside and before I could say anything, she added. "Let me tell you about all these folders. Russ told me the best way to get you started was to pull out the ownership information and all the latest financial information on the live businesses that Russ is involved with. This is what I could find on them."

She leaned over and picked up a sheet of paper and handed it to me. "These are instructions on how to get to the shared file I set up for this project. I moved as many electronic files as I could find into it. I summarized everything here in the computer and printed a copy for you. It's in the first file that's labeled, Biz Summary. I would start with that and then pick a business, find the files for it, and 'dig in'."

"By the way, the password for the Internet is RussandZ, capital R and capital Z."

As she talked, I was thinking... *Wow... there sure are a lot of files here...*

My answer to all this was a tentative. "Okay. I think I've got it." Then I headed over to the chair behind the desk to sit down.

I think Diana sensed my apprehension. She smiled. "I will be right next door if you have any questions. I know at the beginning, it's a bit much. I thought that too when I first started helping Russ."

"Yeah, the pile is a bit bigger than I was expecting."

Diana laughed, "True. Russ once explained it all to me by saying about himself 'I am a sucker for a deal.' Which I think means he got into more businesses than maybe he should have."

With that advice, she gave me a wave that was probably as silly as the one I gave her a couple of minutes earlier and went back to her office.

I pulled out my Iphone and looked at the time, 10:10. *Guess I should get started before I waste any more of the day.*

I picked up the summery sheet. The first line was '#1 Restaurants'. Under that indented was 'A. Ronnie's Ranch - INV – live'. Under that was 'B. 39 Grove – dead'. And under that, 'C. Murphy's Landing Kansas City – dead'. And then '#2 Travel'...

The summary 'sheet' was four sheets of paper stapled together. And when I turned to the last page it had '#15 Insurance'. Each category had between two and five items, except for '#12 Real Estate', which had what looked like fifteen items.

I remember thinking it was a long list. But the mitigating factor was that it also looked like two-thirds of the entries were marked dead. *That will help...*

I looked at the left-hand pile of files in front of me. The top folder was labeled Ronnie's Ranch. Diana was just as efficient as she appeared. *#1 A is on top, of course...*

I picked up the Ronnie's Ranch folder and started to read. Turned out Ronnie's Ranch was a $50,000 investment that Russ had made in 2001 in a Southern California fast food restaurant specializing in 'chicken-fried steak' sandwiches, a confusing name for breaded beef. Anyway, the venture had grown to eight locations in seven years, and Russ's dividends were now $10,000 for the last year. Not a big deal, but the dividends had only been $5,000 the year prior and a note from the company CEO predicted they should be over $20,000 the next year.

After reading all of the Ronnie's Ranch information and deciding it had turned out to be a good investment for Uncle Russ, I was still wondering... *Why did he ever invest in this? How did he hear about it? Why take the risk? His first two restaurant investments failed, so why invest in this one?*

As I went through the pile, the different company files were both fascinating and a bit of a puzzle. I made notes of questions to ask later. I was soon deep into my reading.

I was 'powering through' my sixth company when I heard a knock at the door. It was Diana standing in my open doorway. "Hey, I'm going to have a sandwich before I head up to San Francisco. Want to join me?"

I had no idea how long I had been working or what time it was. I simply said. "Ah... Sure. Sounds good." I popped up from my desk.

We headed down to a quiet kitchen, and I figured out Anna must have stayed out after dropping the kids at their school in Portola Valley. We were alone in the house.

I had never done anything in the kitchen before, so Diana gave me instructions on where the things were -- bread, drinks, plates, etc. and she got out most of the rest.

I made a turkey and Swiss cheese sandwich, put a handful of Fritos on my plate, and added an apple. Diana suggested we sit at the 'eating counter' which had four stools. I put my plate there and sat down.

Diana sat next to me, "So how were your first three hours?"

I thought for a second. "It is more interesting than I thought it would be. All the businesses are different, and with the notes from the people running them, you really get to see what their main problems are. How did he get into so many different kinds of companies?"

"I asked him that one day. He told me it was two things. One was that he was a numbers person, so his contribution was building spreadsheets and business models and figuring out the strategy of how each company made the most money. So it didn't matter what the company did. He just needed to understand its numbers. And the second reason was he occasionally taught a course at the Stanford Business School. Some of his students had projects and asked him to get involved." Then, she added, "As Russ would say… 'And that was that'."

I watched her as she talked. She had this cute way of pushing her hair out of the way with one hand while using the other hand to make a point. Like when she made the point about Russ, she used one finger to emphasize that we were on point one and then two fingers when she talked about point two.

"It does seem he has the simplest way of explaining how things work out." I said. I was still looking at her without eating.

"Oh, you have no idea." She said. "He has ideas about nearly everything. All you have to do is ask. Working here is like working no other place. You'll see."

Then she added, "I'm really going to miss it."

What did she say??? Is she leaving? Am I really just replacing her?

"You're... ah... going to miss it here? Why is that?"

"Didn't I tell you? Sorry. At the end of the summer, I'm going back to school. I have about six months left here, and I'm already having 'withdrawal pains'. You'll see."

"It is not just the setting," she continued. "Although this farm could not be much better for me, it's the whole dynamic that Russ has with everyone around him. I... ah... I have learned so much about people. How they think. What makes them happy. Just a little bit of everything. You'll see."

That is the third time she has said 'you'll see'... It is almost mysterious the way she says it...

"How long have you been here?" It was now the only question I could think of.

"Almost two years. I graduated from college, went to Europe for six weeks, and then came straight here. I was only going to stay one year, but after six months I knew that I really wanted to stay for another one. I asked Stanford if I could push back my start for a year there, and they said 'yes'."

Hmmmm... so she is only 24 - 25... younger than she acts...

"So you are going to go to Stanford in the fall. That isn't too far away. You can come and visit."

"I'm counting on it... my way of getting a little bit more of Russ while I'm at school."

She waited a few seconds and then added, "Have you figured out why you are here yet?"

I wasn't sure I heard her question right as it seemed to be something she already knew. So I tentatively answered, "You mean my helping with getting all the paperwork straightened up."

"No, not that." She replied "It is more like, what does Russ think you will get out of spending three months here. He seems to have a knack of knowing what a person needs and trying to help them find it. Keep that in mind, and maybe you'll figure it out."

With that, she finished her sandwich. Mine was only half eaten, and I hadn't touched my chips or my apple.

Diana stood up and took her plate to the dishwasher. "Well, I have to run or I will be late. Even early on Friday afternoons, the traffic into the city can be slow. I will see you Monday before noon."

Caught with my mouth full of food once again, I chewed as fast as I could… "Have a nice weekend."

"You too," she called back over her shoulder as she started to climb the stairs. Then she stopped and turned around. "Estelle and Charlotte will be here this weekend. Extra good luck then.

I wasn't sure I had heard her right. "Extra good luck?"

"Well, you have not met the twins, but you might need extra luck. Maybe not… you can let me know." And then up the stairs she went.

I wonder what that is all about…

6

I heard the front door close. *Hmmm... all alone in the house.*

I didn't feel like snooping around, but it did feel quiet. Nobody was likely to be home until three o'clock at the earliest, so I could wander around a bit.

As I finished my sandwich and chips, I thought...*I know what Russ thinks I need... I just need to get over Rachel...* I was wrong about that.

I grabbed my apple and put my plate in the dishwasher. I bounced the apple in my hand and went to look at the books on the bookshelves near the fireplace. I recognized certain classics like; *Count of Monte Cristo, A Tale of Two Cities...* then more current authors like Grisham and Clancy... and then saw a bunch of books on physics, history, biographies, and religion.

He reads 'everything'... except for business... hmmm...

I took a bite of my apple and started back to my office. Then I decided to take a detour and visit the game room instead.

I wandered more slowly through the room this time. It was better than the Discovery Zone I went to when I was a kid. The two bowling lanes and the basketball half court put this room over the top.

I spun one of the men on the foosball table and went over to the art and crafts area. There were two sinks, easels and a wall full of supplies. My high school art teacher would have loved it. The arcade-sized video games included Ms Pac Man and Galaxy, two of my childhood favorites. The big screen Wii area looked great. Actually, the whole room was amazing… I hoped I would have an excuse to spend time here.

I was heading back to my office when a text message arrived on my phone. It was from Don White, the Vice President and General Council at Fair Way Markets. Fair Way was the client I had worked on the most at my old law firm.

The message was short and direct, typical Don White. "Call me this afternoon if you can. 312-455-4191."

I wondered what he wanted. It was probably a question about something I did on his account a couple of months ago. *But why isn't someone from the firm calling? Must be my old boss is trying to avoid another confrontation...* Just thinking of him put a bitter feeling into my brain.

Still, I had liked Don White and Fair Way. Don had grown up as an inner city kid who got a football scholarship to Notre Dame. He had been good enough at football to get drafted in the NFL and for four years in the offseason, he went to law school and got his law degree. It turned out to be fortunate timing as it was the same time he graduated that he was released from the Chicago Bears.

He had worked at the same law firm as I had, and three years ago went to work at one of his clients, Fair Way. Fair Way had developed a few niche online marketplaces that were growing very quickly. Lucky for Don, they were expected to file for an IPO later this year.

Back at my desk, I dialed the number to find out what Don needed. After a couple of minutes of the usual personal catch-up talk, Don got to the point. "I called to offer you a job here at Fair Way."

A job? Where did that come from?

He continued with his pitch, "You know we've been thinking of an IPO later this year. It hasn't been announced yet, but we met with some bankers this week, and they felt we were ready, so we are moving forward."

"With that and our continued growth, we feel we will need another full-time lawyer on staff. You know us, and we know you. I think it would be a perfect fit."

He paused. I felt he was waiting for my response. Before I could say anything he continued. I think he sensed a bit of hesitation from me, which was true.

"I know this comes out of the blue for you, but I want to add that financially it would be a very good offer. Your base would be higher than you were getting before, your guaranteed bonus would be 30% of the base and you would get a nice amount of pre-IPO stock options."

I knew from my short work experience that this was exactly the job offer many two-to-four-year associates at big law firms dream about getting. Also, I knew that Don was aware that he was making me a 'plum' job offer. This time I had to answer his pause. I had been trained in how to react in legal settings and negotiations. But that was easier to do for a client. This was me and my career and… my life.

"Wow, Don. You're right. It is 'out of the blue'." *First agree with them. Then stall… but be direct. Don likes people who are decisive and direct.* "You know I love Fair Way and working with you. How much time do I have to commit?"

"I know you just got out there, so I can give you until a week from Monday to commit, and I can give you another two weeks to start. I will send the detailed offer letter to you by Tuesday."

"Thanks Don. The timing sounds fair enough."

"Jay, we really want you here, so shoot me any questions you have when you get the offer."

"I will. Knowing you, it will be spelled out so even I can understand it." I tried to end the call with a bit of humor.

Don laughed. Then he used my humor to push me even harder. "See, you know me so well that we have to have you here."

I laughed and then added. "I will call with any questions."

"Have a great weekend, Jay."

"You too, Don."

We hung up and my mind went into overdrive. *Now what do I do?...*

I was a bit paralyzed with my thoughts. They ranged from a 'once in a lifetime opportunity' -- to the fact that I had made a three-month commitment to Russ -- to this offer could open up a new career path -- to I just got to California -- and then I really had no idea what I wanted to

Also at this point, I still really had no idea 'why' I was here. The answers to the 'Why me? Why now?' questions from the start of 'my adventure' were still as murky and mysterious as ever. Yet the people here were already becoming special to me, and this was just my second day ...*How did that happen?*

After a few minutes, I decided I had basically ten days to make up my mind and that maybe the best thing to do now was to settle down by not thinking about it. So I spent the next several hours in my office reviewing Russ's online and paper files, making notes of the questions I had. I was so focused I did not hear the front door open. But I did hear Anna...

"Alex, before you start playing, I need help bringing in all the food. You know the drill. Food first, play later."

I could hear the kids shouting to each other even if I could not understand them. I decided the thing to do was to volunteer and help. I saw Anna heading down the stairs with a couple of bags.

"Anna, can I help?"

Without pausing she called back, "That would be great. There are lots of bags in the back of the car."

I went to the SUV parked in front of the house with its hatchback open. The back was piled high with bags from a couple of different stores. Apparently, Anna had spent much of the day stocking up on food for the coming week. I grabbed as many bags as I could carry and headed down to the kitchen. Alex ran past me out to the car to get more.

In the kitchen, Anna was busy unpacking all the bags and sorting things to be put away. "Thanks Jay. Put the bags on any empty counter space."

"No problem."

"If you could help with the rest of the stuff, I would greatly appreciate it. I will unpack it all… we have a big crowd this weekend."

I went upstairs wondering who the big crowd was. Two twin 16-year old girls just didn't seem to be a big crowd to me. Alex and I brought most of the bags in with a bit of distracted help from Alicia and Kevin.

I dropped the last bag on the counter and told Anna it was the last. Alex looked at me and said. "One quick game of air hockey?"

"Ah… sure." I followed him to the game room with the full expectation of playing one game and then going back to my office and pushing through more files.

I was looking forward to a game of air hockey. I had not played in five years, but my last game was winning my fraternity's air hockey tournament. So I was good at this…

Alex turned the game on, and the air flowed out from all the little holes in the playing surface. He slid one of the little plastic mallets to my side of the table and offered, "You want to warm up a bit?"

"Yes. It has been a few years since I last played, so some warm-up would be good."

We banged the little plastic puck back and forth a bit. I stopped it on my side a couple of times to practice a serve. After a minute or two I said,

"I'm ready."

Alex slid the puck to me. "Guests serve first." Having first serve I knew was a tiny advantage in air hockey.

If you have never played air hockey, the objective is to get the small plastic puck past the opponent's mallet and into a 10-inch slot at the back of the opponent's side of the table. The first player to score seven points wins. Arcade style machines have electronic scoring to eliminate any arguments. This was a full-size arcade table.

I will just hit a couple of soft shots and see how good Alex is... I want him to have fun...

That is what I did. Alex blocked/returned each of my shots, so I stepped up my pace a bit... and so did he.

Thunk

It is the sound the puck makes after it goes into the slot and falls into a small holder down below the table.

Alex 1 – Jay 0

"Nice shot." I said. In air hockey, almost all talking is done between points as the focus during playing a point can be intense.

We played a bit more.

Thunk

Alex 2 – Jay 0

I started to realize he was much better than the average kid. When you get scored upon, the puck comes at your end, and you get to serve again.

A good serve can be very important in air hockey. If you can get a good flow going on your attack, you can sometimes score before your opponent has time to slow the puck down for a counter attack. I had won many games with my serve. I decided I needed a couple of scores to make a 'game' out of it.

I came out with one of my best serves, which was basically a fake down the middle, but actually a bounce shot to the left.

Thunk

Alex 2 – Jay 1

Alex just smiled, as he got the puck out to serve it.

Thunk

Alex 3 – Jay 1

His serve was almost identical to mine… I wondered if it was a fluke.

So I served again. This time he blocked my serve, but I knocked the rebound in.

Thunk

Alex 3 – Jay 2

We battled back and forth a bit with both of us doing as good a defense as possible. Soon it was Alex 6 – Jay 5 and my serve.

I hit a perfect serve.

Thunk

Alex 6 – Jay 6

Next point wins, with Alex serving… Perfect…

Thunk

Alex 7 – Jay 6

Alex smiled and said. "Want to play best out of seven?"

"Sure." I was in heaven. I loved playing air hockey in college and to play someone at the same level was the best way to enjoy the game.

Alex beat me four games to two. At least I won two.

Six games of air hockey, and I was sweating, my shirt was untucked and…

"There you are." It was Uncle Russ up on the balcony. "Looks like you two have been having fun."

Before I could answer, Alex chimed in, "GP. He's pretty good. I think he could beat you."

Russ was coming down the stairs. "Is he good enough to beat you?"

"Maybe," Alex responded, "but not today." His smile was growing.

"I'm not sure ever," I added.

"Jay, your mother tells me you played high school basketball. Is that true?" Russ was at the bottom of the stairs and heading toward the basketball area.

"I did, but it was a long time ago."

"Well Alex has a game tomorrow and if you have the time, I'm sure he could benefit from any tips you could give him." Russ had taken a basketball from a rack holding six or seven balls. He took a three-point shot. It bounced off the front rim. "Hate when I'm short."

Alex was still standing next to me. "Would you watch me shoot and see if you notice anything I could improve?"

"Sure".

I asked Alex about his own skills and about his teammates. The three of us spent the next hour going over the different angles to drive with and a lot of what I had learned to do when I played. It was great to watch Alex 'soak up' as much as he could and try to do the moves I asked him to try. And then put a big smile on when he was able to 'pull it off'.

Anna finally interrupted us with a 30-minute warning before dinner.

I excused myself, saying I needed a quick shower and a change of clothes. I did both as quickly as possible to be back to 'the kitchen' a little early this time. I was five minutes early as I walked in from the patio, but still everyone else was there, except Alicia. Anna had put out chips, veggies, and dips. Everyone seemed to be happily 'chowing down'.

Russ introduced me to his two twin granddaughters. Although genetically identical, they could not have been more different.

Estelle was dressed and made up, easily '16 going on 24'. Charlotte was all in black in a conservative Goth outfit. Estelle's hair was long and blond. Charlotte's was short and black. I doubted either color was natural.

Both girls had brought a girlfriend with them, and each was dressed like the twin they were with. Estelle smiled and tried to look sexy when I was introduced. Charlotte was civil, but acted like it was basically a waste of time to meet me. The two friends were fully polite and shook hands.

Anna had announced it was burger night, so people started to line up. Estelle and her guest first, then Charlotte and her friend. Then Alex and Kevin. And finally, Russ and me. Alicia did appear and went to the back of the line next to me. She tugged at my sleeve and asked. "We still good for 10 AM tomorrow?"

I smiled at her and said, "Absolutely".

"Good," she said. "I called the stable and reserved Bronco and Chestnut for you and me. You'll like Chestnut. She is a big horse, but very gentle, and she will not run unless you want her to."

"That sounds perfect for me."

Again, Anna's food presentation was organized and neat. I took so long picking what to put on my burger and what to add to the plate (potato salad, fruit salad, and baked beans) that when I got to the table, only one chair was left between Alicia and Anna. I took it.

The meal went fine with people discussing various topics. The twins and their friends were also going riding in the morning, but they weren't starting until noon Alex had his basketball game against the best team in his league. We talked mostly what movie to watch tonight in the theater.

Then Alicia spoke up. "I have my Word."

"Go right ahead," Russ said.

"We are studying the Revolution, and I have to write a report about part of the Declaration of Independence. The part I am assigned is the part that goes 'life, liberty, and the pursuit of happiness'. I can handle the first two, but what does 'pursuit of happiness' really mean."

Before Russ or anyone else could speak, Charlotte blurted out in a sarcastic tone. "Aren't we the perfect little student working on school reports on a Friday night. You need more friends."

Without skipping a beat, Alicia looked right back at her and said, "At least I'm not like you, in your room watching porn on the Internet so you can practice getting better at oral sex."

Holy shit... did she just say that? ....

Charlotte sat there with her mouth open for a second and then said, "You little snoop. Are you spying on me?"

Russ held up his hand for silence which he immediately got. I think most of the rest of us were unprepared to say anything anyway. Although, I could see smirks on Estelle and her friend's faces.

"I think that is enough on that topic. After dinner, I want both of you to apologize to Jay and Anna for disturbing their meal time. I would ask you to apologize to each other, but I do not want you to lie to each other to do so." He continued, "At some point Charlotte, I would like to have a short conversation on sex as a way to become popular. And Alicia, I think a similar short talk on respecting privacy would be good as well."

Charlotte wanted to look defiant, but Russ stared straight at her until she finally looked down. Alicia was already looking down.

"Just so you two aren't feeling too bad, when I was your age, the only pornography we could get was *Playboy Magazine,* and we worked hard to get an issue. And my older sister got so tired of me ratting her out to our parents, that she started calling me Little Rat as a nickname."

Charlotte was now looking up again, and Alicia actually smiled at the Little Rat comment.

"As for your Word, Alicia, it is one of my favorite lines in history." Russ was back in form now. "Thomas Jefferson wrote it and never defined it. He started by saying that every human was endowed by our creator with certain inalienable rights, including those three. And remember, that life and liberty part was written by a guy who had over 100 slaves at the time… So who knows what he really meant."

"However, let's see if we can give it meaning today. The pursuit part is easy. Right, Alex?"

Alex, who had been listening intently, was still a bit startled to be called on. "Ah… it just means we have the right to go after our own happiness, I guess."

"Yes, it's pretty simple, although it does point out that when your pursuit of happiness conflicts with mine that is where all of politics lays. Like a property owner's right to right to control and keep his or her property private and the rights of a group of surfers to gain access to a public surfing beach that can only be accessed over other's private property… who wins, who compromises and who loses is the core of what is politics…"

That is an odd example…

"But the more interesting word is happiness. Anyone want to give a try at defining happiness or what it is to be happy?"

There was silence.

Kevin finally offered, "It's when you feel good about what's going on around you."

"That's good Kevin." Russ smiled at the nine-year-old. "My guess is we all know what being happy feels like, it's one of those things that is really hard to put into words. Let's see if we can break this idea down a bit."

Just like last night... Russ is breaking things down...

"I think you will find that there are two kinds of happiness. One comes from what Kevin said, the situation around you. Like when Alex beat Jay at air hockey. It was obvious he felt happy about that."

Alex's grin got twice as big.

"Some situational happiness lasts longer than others." Russ looked at Estelle, adding, "Like when the cute boy you have been admiring looks at you and smiles. For a brief moment you feel happy. Of course if he never calls, then that happiness will fade. But if he does call, you feel more happiness. But if the first date does not go well, then happiness fades."

Now everyone was looking at Russ. His examples had them understanding the concept.

"The other kind of happiness I call True Happiness. Not because it is any better than situational happiness, but because it is usually more long lasting. True Happiness is greatly influenced by how you feel about yourself and the life you are leading. I do not mean like being celebrities and rich people. I mean people who are happy with what they do all day. The McDonald's drive-up window clerk, who is proud of her ability to get four out of five of her customers to smile when she gives them their food. Maybe it's the nice things she says to them like, 'I like your car' or 'your dog is so cute' or 'I like the big box of McNuggets too'."

"She goes home happy. She wakes up in the morning happy. You may say that she is weird, that she is just a McDonald's clerk." Russ paused. "But as you know happiness is an internal feeling and if she is happy with what she does, then by definition she is truly happy."

Kevin spoke up. "Wouldn't she be happier at In and Out Burger? I read they pay better."

Russ smiled and turned toward Kevin again. "Another good question, Kevin." "As it turns out there have been many studies on the topic of money, material things and happiness. The results almost always indicate that once you are making enough to feed and shelter your family in safety, then the amount of money you have above that has very little to do with happiness. My personal addition to the topic would be to say that money can buy quick happiness. But every time you buy quick happiness the next time, you have to buy more of whatever it was to achieve a happy state again."

"So in essence, money is a 'no win game' when it comes to happiness."

Estelle waited for Russ to finish then asked, "But you can buy someone else's happiness, right?"

"I think it's pretty much the same answer. Let's say your mother buys you a new Camaro – that would be cool and make you happy."

Estelle smiled, "Yes and it is a good idea."

"That may be, but in a couple months the newness will wear off, and so that 'fancy car' will just be 'your car'... no happiness added. So now your mother buys you a new BMW. Happy again?"

"Yup.

"But this feeling too will soon wear off. So now we are at Ferrari levels... Get the point?"

"Got it."

"So back to True Happiness." Russ paused again. "As I said, it is internal. The nice thing about internal happiness is that you depend on no other person or event for that happiness.

"One way to look at these two kinds of happiness is to use waves and a beach. We can make the waves our situational happiness events. They come in and they raise our happiness, but then it wears out and our happiness goes back down. True Happiness is like a rising tide or water level. The general level is higher the waves are just added on top of it.

Of course, unlike ocean tides you hope that your internal happiness stays at a high level…"

Russ continued, "I hope I haven't confused you with all of this. Alicia, you look a bit confused."

"I am not confused about what you said, just confused on what to write in my report," Alicia explained.

Russ tried again. "So I'm not sure what Thomas Jefferson was thinking when he wrote those words. But if he was thinking of the two types of happiness, then he would want you to have equal access to situational happiness and also the ability to have access to True Happiness. If you write something like that, I think your teacher will like your thought process."

As Russ had talked, I noticed that everyone ate less and less until at the end everyone was just staring straight at him, even Charlotte...

Since Russ noticed the silence and he knew he was finished. He said, "Kevin can you pass me the chips. They would help my situational happiness right now." There were a couple of laughs and the table went back to normal eating.

The next topic was what movie would play in the theater. The twins actually agreed on something, watching an old John Hughes movie. They narrowed it down to *Breakfast Club* or *Pretty and Pink*. Charlotte pushed a bit for *Breakfast*

Club which they hadn't seen in a long time and the two guests had never seen. Alex, Alicia, and Kevin invited themselves to join them.

It was Alex's night to help Anna with clean-up, so the others said they would set everything up in the theater, but asked him to hurry. They each grabbed three or four of Anna's freshly baked Chocolate Chip cookies and went to the theater.

Russ once again offered me berries and ice cream. Once again, I said 'yes'.

When we were settled at the fireplace, Russ asked, "Everything okay in the cottage?"

"Yeah... I overslept this morning though. It is so quiet there."

"That's good. With the kids in the house, school mornings can get pretty noisy."

We both took a moment to enjoy a big spoonful of berries and ice cream. I finished mine first, so I commented about the discussion at dinner.

"Interesting way to approach Thomas Jefferson and The Declaration of Independence."

"Ah... happiness is one of my favorite topics. It was a great opening to tell five of my grandchildren a simple way to think of being happy in your life."

"They seemed to be following your thinking."

"I noticed that as well and was surprised they actually listened. Especially after Charlotte and Alicia…" Russ paused for a second. "Just FYI, those two have had a history like that now for about two years. I worry that Charlotte is having trouble growing up." Russ paused again.

"I mentioned it to her mother, who seems oblivious. I'm not sure what to do. When Monique and her husband divorced four years ago, Charlotte took the brunt as she was closer to her Dad than her mother… And Monique was difficult for me while she was growing up. I probably spent twice as much time with her as Mark and Katlin, and in the end, I am not sure I did a very good job. I think I misunderstood her most of the time. I talked when I should have been listening. I treated her the same as the other two, when in reality she is much different. I tried to guide her to be like her brother and sister. That was my mistake.

He looked like he was in serious thought at that moment. I didn't really know what to say so I weakly added, "That can be tough."

He seemed to snap back and a smile returned to his face.

I wonder what he was thinking about just then?

"Yes, life always has its tough moments, but it has its fun moments too. I am not sure kids can really understand that. They do not give much credit to fun, since they have so much of it." Then he added, "It was like today for you."

Me? Today? What is he talking about?

"You put in some hours working and then had fun with Alex. How do you feel about today?"

I thought for a second, I had had a very good day so I said so. "I had a great day, but I also found reading your business files interesting."

"I guess my point would be that you feel much better about today – much happier if I can use that word – having the combination of work and fun."

He continued, "I think too often people put fun and work completely into separate places. The week is work, and the weekend is fun. I think it puts too much pressure on the weekend. If you plan some fun during the week and maybe do a bit of work on the weekend, you'll have an overall better feeling about your life. An increase in True Happiness to use my language from dinner. Of course, making work fun is another important concept, but we can hit that idea another night."

I was thinking how logical this all seemed. I was also surprised that no one had ever made that point to me before. "Sounds right, I have just never thought about it before."

Russ looked at me a second and then said, "I think that is normal. I think most people are so busy living their lives that they do not have the time to figure out a lot of things about themselves and their lives... Try adding at least an hour of fun or at least some relaxation that you enjoy. I know that some television can be fun or relaxing, but not very much of it. It's so passive that most people's brains get almost nothing from the experience. Jay, do you read books much?

"Not as much as I used to," I answered, thinking... *Where is this going?*

"Well I have found that unlike television, books stimulate the mind, force you to think or at least use your imagination. What I like best about books is you can enjoy them almost anywhere for almost any amount of time, either a few minutes or hours, which in my view makes books a great source of fun and relaxation... and in some cases a lot of learning as well."

I didn't have a good response, so I asked, "How do you pick a book to read?"

"For me it's become easy. I have a couple of fiction writers that write what I call 'airplane books'... books that can be read usually in a five-hour flight. Like Dick Francis or John Grisham. I like their stories. Then I also read topics I like. For those, I look online for what is new and read a few reviews.

"I also bought the new Amazon Kindle last year. Works great." He reached down on the lower shelf of the table next to his chair and pulled out a small screen device and handed it to me. "The nice thing about electronic books is that I can buy them, put them in my Kindle and then, if I read the first twenty pages, and I am not enjoying them, I simply start the next one. I do not feel the urge to finish them simply because otherwise I wasted the paper and trees... so electronic books have made me a more discerning reader."

He took the last bite of his ice cream... I had finished mine while listening to him. He looked at his watch and announced, "I need another early night. I promised Alex I would go surfing with him early tomorrow before we head 'over the hill' to his basketball game."

He surfs at 68??

"As I recall, you have riding with Alicia."

"Yes I do, but we do not meet up until 10, so I have some extra time. Maybe I will go online and find a good book." I smiled.

Russ stood up. "Sounds good. Take my Kindle and try it out. And have fun with Alicia tomorrow. Just remember she's twelve going on twenty-two." He smiled.

I gave him what must have been a quizzical expression, because he then added. "You'll see soon enough."

What is it with this family and all the 'you'll sees' anyway? Then I thought… *Diana was right about the twins. They were already high maintenance, and all we had going on tonight was dinner.*

We cleared our bowls, I said good night, headed out the patio door and down the lit pathway to my cottage.

Good old number 6 should show up soon. I thought. This time, I had remembered to leave a light on. Once inside, I went immediately over to my journal and started writing about my day and Russ's thoughts. It took me almost an hour to get it all down. I started thinking how full my day had been even though I was staying out in this isolated farm near nothing.

Another great day… interesting I feel happy about the day when in truth, nothing really happened… why is that?….

I thought a bit more about Russ's comments about happiness, especially True Happiness.

I wonder how true all of that is? I will have to pay more attention and see what I can figure out...

And then it hit me. The Don White offer call had been just this afternoon.

How could I have forgotten that?

I found it odd that I had been so focused on Russ's files, then Russ's grandchildren, and then Russ's thoughts on happiness that I had not once thought about Don White and the Fair Way offer.

Does that mean I don't care about the offer?... or does it mean more that I have found myself surrounded by an environment here I find totally captivating?

It was a good question, but once again I decided to delay thinking more about it.

I got out Russ's Kindle to see if he had downloaded anything I wanted to read. I found it was just like his book shelves, nearly 30 books on all sorts of different topics... *what would be good to read now?* Then I saw two Dick Francis book covers. I had never heard the name before. I picked the one titled *Bolt.* Ten minutes later I was washed up and in bed, reading.

7

I woke up with Russ's Kindle right next to my pillow. I must have fallen asleep reading… I don't think I read more than 20 pages. I had been pretty tired again.

This morning the clock only read 8:15, so I was getting better. I figured I could get to the kitchen a little after nine and have a nice leisurely breakfast.

Russ said that Saturday mornings Anna may or may not have anything prepared, so I best leave time to make something myself.

First, though, I called my mom. I had called her when I drove through San Francisco two days ago, so she knew I made it out here safely. But yesterday had been so busy, I forgot to call again.

We talked for twenty minutes about my first two days. She said I sounded pretty good. I told her that I was doing better, partly because I was so busy and partly because the environment was so different. I decided not to tell her about the Fair Way offer. I was not ready to have a serious conversation about it.

After I hung up, I realized I was 'down' a bit. Hearing my mother's voice had triggered memories of my past with Rachel.

That will pass... hopefully.

I showered and shaved slowly. I love when a shower has a great spray, and this shower had exactly the kind of spray I love. Strong, wide and not too pin-like.

I dressed, added a t-shirt under my shirt, and a fleece jacket as Russ told me it could be cold for part of the ride. It was now 9:30 and I was slipping a bit behind schedule. When I got to the kitchen, I saw Anna with Alicia. Alicia yelled to me, "What kind of sandwiches do you like? I'm making lunch for us."

Guess we're going out for a long ride...

"Do you have some turkey and Swiss cheese?"

"Yes we do. Lettuce, mayo, tomato?"

"All three... And good morning to you, Anna."

"Good morning, we have pancakes and bacon this morning, do you care for any?"

"They both sound great."

"Go sit down. There is apple juice and orange juice in the two pitchers. I'll have the pancakes done in two minutes. Do you want two or three?"

Decisions, decisions... I am going riding, so...

"Three sounds perfect."

There was no one at the table, so I picked a place near the pitchers. Almost before I had decided which kind of juice to have, (orange), Anna put a plate with three huge pancakes and four pieces of bacon on it before me.

I should have asked how big before I said three...

"Wow, Anna, these are huge."

"That's how we make 'em at Casa Russ. You're a growing boy. I'm sure you will have no trouble finishing them."

I poured syrup on the top one and dug in. They tasted great. I ate in silence, while Alicia continued her lunch preparations and asked Anna on how to cut things, etc.

Alicia asked me, "What do you want to drink? Water, soda, or juice?"

"Ah... water sounds good."

I was just finishing my second pancake when Alicia put a funny two-sided bag over one of the chairs and sat down.

"Okay. We are set to go whenever you finish."

No pressure here...I should have ordered only two, but it had been a long time since I had such delicious pancakes and real maple syrup...

I dug into the last one and ate as fast as I could. I offered Alicia a strip of bacon as well

"No thanks, I don't like bacon. It's not really good for you."

"No it isn't, but then a lot of things aren't good for you. You just like them. Just don't eat too much of the bad stuff, and you'll be all right." I finished, put my plate in the dishwasher and met Alicia by the patio door.

We headed down the path toward the cottages, and she took a quick left through a break in a hedge. On the other side was a small parking area with five golf carts and one ATV parked there.

Alicia went to the closest cart, unplugged it, threw her bag in the back, hopped in the driver's seat and patted the passenger seat next to her.

"Hop in."

She's driving... but she's only twelve. Right??

I hesitated.

"Come on. I have been driving these since I was ten. You'll be fine. Anyway all the carts have seat belts and GP makes all of us kids wear them. You can wear it if you're nervous."

She buckled up, put the golf cart into reverse and off we went. I didn't buckle up, but I did reach for the handle near the roof to balance when we made some sharp turns.

The parking lot intersected with the road that went down past the cottages. I looked at Number 6 as we went by it.

Home…. Hmm three days and that is 'home'.

The ride to the stables was four or five miles. Sometimes we were on open hills with an occasional big old oak tree, and sometimes we rode through an almost dark forest with towering redwood trees blotting out the sun. The sun was also partially obscured by the mist/fog that got thicker the closer we got to the coast.

It turned out Alicia was an excellent driver. No reckless curves or pushing too fast over blind hills. At one point, we came upon a county road that cut across our private road. The golf cart had electronic 'clickers' that opened the gates. Alicia carefully looked both ways before crossing.

We finally crested one small hill and had our first glance of the horse stables. They were larger than I had envisioned. There were three long red stable buildings with slightly slanted roofs, a two-story white farmhouse, and a half dozen other red buildings of different sizes. There were horses in several of the open fields with white split-rail type fences. Past the stables I could see a dirt exercise oval track and a smaller jumping area with several jumps set up.

"It's bigger than I thought," I said as we got closer. "How many horses are here?"

"I don't really know, but I would guess more than a hundred. GP only has ten that we use for riding."

She pulled the golf cart next to the largest red stable. I noticed the same cart charging boxes as back at the house.

"Hi Alicia." A man who looked around forty in a baseball cap with "Giants" on the front, called out as she hopped from the cart.

"Hi Harry," she responded.

"Bronco and Chestnut are in paddock two, ready to go."

"Thanks Harry. I'd like you to meet Jay. He's staying with us for next couple of months. He is coming along, so I can try Bronco on the new course. Then we'll head up to Margie's Peak."

"Nice ride up there. Should be sunny already." Harry put out his hand, "Good to meet you Jay. You'll find Chestnut a totally cooperative horse even for someone new. Have you ridden before?"

"Yes, but it has been ten years."

"For most people, it's like riding a bicycle and in twenty feet you will remember everything. As I said, Chestnut is one of the easiest rides I've known.

Alicia started to walk away, and Harry added, "I lowered the two high jumps one rung when you told me you wanted to do the new course. It should be very doable now."

"Thanks Harry."

We approached what must have been paddock two. A good looking black horse was tied to one of the rails, whining and shaking his head. Alicia ran toward him. As she got closer, the horse calmed a bit, and Alicia climbed up on a rung of the fence and stroked his head.

"Bronco, Bronco. It's only been a week. But I am here now." She reached in her pocket produced a small carrot, and held it out. Bronco took it gently from her. "You sweet boy. I have more of those for you if you behave."

"That's Chestnut over there," she now told me. If you give her this little apple, I think she will like you more." She handed me a small apple.

I walked over to Chestnut. This would be interesting. Chestnut took the whole apple from my hand and began chopping away dropping apple parts all over the ground.

"Jay, can you help me up here." Alicia had opened the gate and was standing next to Bronco.

"Sure." I went over and cupped my hands for her to lift herself up. She had obviously done this move a lot. She was up in the saddle before I knew it.

"Can you get up on Chestnut? Then we can ride over to the course?"

Twelve going on twenty-two... I was starting to understand Russ's comment from last night.

Chestnut and I stood quietly and watched Alicia and Bronco do a couple of circuits of the jumps. I was no jump expert, but they looked totally fluid together. No hesitation, no awkward moments. After the second circuit, Alicia rode Bronco toward me and Chestnut.

"Thanks for waiting. Harry changed the course this week and I really wanted to try it. Now let me show you the trail to Margie's Peak. I think you'll like it."

The ride up was fun. Sometimes single file, and sometimes the trail was wide enough to ride next to each other. Alicia told me about her school, her feud with Charlotte which she confirmed was almost two years old now. She asked about my mother. She asked if I had a girlfriend. She asked why I had come here. She asked anything that came into her mind. I gave her straight forward answers, but without all the 'gory' details.

After an hour of riding, we had climbed up above the fog into the sunlight. We stopped, and I reached in my pocket and put on my hat and sunglasses – last night Alicia had reminded me to bring them. I took off my fleece and stuffed it in one of the saddle bags. We entered another redwood grove and the way got steep for a while. We walked slowly and Chestnut picked her footing carefully.

Then we entered a clearing with a stunning view. We were above the fog like being above the clouds in an airplane. We headed to the edge of the hill where I saw a picnic table.

"Tie Chestnut to the branch over there and then come here. I have our lunch bags."

Twelve going on twenty-two...

She jumped off Bronco, tied him up, came over to the picnic table, and unpacked lunch. Two sandwiches for me, an apple, a bag of nuts and water.

"I love it here," she said.

"It is spectacular. Why is it called Margie's Peak?"

"Margie' was GPs first wife and my grandmother. It was her favorite spot on the Farm."

First wife... there has been more than one then?

"Do you still see your grandmother?

"Oh no. She died over thirty years ago. I think in a crash or something like that. GP keeps a nice photo of her in his office."

There was silence for a moment and then she asked me, "How do you like the Farm so far?"

"So far it's a pretty special place."

"It is."

"What is your favorite thing about the Farm?" I was thinking she might say Bronco based on her excitement when she saw him.

"I like that there are no rules here."

No rules here??? ...

"No rules?" I asked.

"GP says the Farm is a 'no rules' zone, just respect. He says society needs laws, but people don't need rules. All they should do is respect themselves and others and everything else will follow. And it usually does."

Wow... what a basic concept, and she even gets it.

"How does that work in reality?"

She gave me a funny look. "Before you do something, you think about what it will look like. Am I respecting myself and am I respecting others...? Don't get me wrong. We still make lots of mistakes, but respect makes you feel in control of your own actions. That makes the Farm seem like a sanctuary for me, except of course, when Charlotte is here. But then I just try to avoid her as much as I can."

"And how does the 'no rules' idea work when you're only nine, like Kevin?"

"Kevin is a special case. He's fine with the no rules - respect thing. His problem is more school and social skills in general."

"He seems fine to me."

"Ah... yes. He does fine with the family. Plus you're not nine. Or even twelve. Kevin can be very intimidating. He is just too smart." She stopped there.

Kevin? Intimidating? He is quite bright for a nine-year old. After all, he tried to hire me the moment we met.

"Too bright? How does that work?"

Alicia thought for a minute and then said, "It causes all kinds of problems. He is reading books most of his friends won't read until high school, if ever. His questions in class are ones only the teacher understands. It makes him difficult to talk to if you're nine like he is. And then there is math."

"Math?"

"Yeah, he is some kind of math genius. I watch him do it. and I can't figure it all out. Two months ago the school put him in my math class – at age nine – and my class is a year advanced. so we are doing 7th grade math. Anyway he has only been in the class two months and he is about to finish our book. Then they will move him up one more class this year. It takes him two months to do what it takes me nine months."

She continued. "I heard Mom and Dad talking about it one time. The school felt it was better to have him in a class environment even if he speeds past everyone. But it does leads to problems. No one in my class can really be his friend. At least, they don't tease him or treat him badly like some of the nine year olds do. His regular classmates are completely intimidated by him mentally, so they pick on him socially."

Twelve going on twenty-two… and has a complete psychological appraisal of her brother.

"So what does GP say about this?" I was using the GP name for the first time, and it seemed like the right thing to do with Alicia.

"He does what does for all of us. He listens to us and gives us ways of thinking about the circumstances of our lives and how to best - 'navigate reality' - as he says."

Alicia stood up, gathered our plastic bags into one paper bag and put it into one of her 'saddle bags'. She headed over to Bronco, started talking to him and gave him two small carrots. He lit up at her kindness.

"Can you give me a lift up again?"

I did and then got back on Chestnut and we headed down the hill. Going down was slower, as the horses had to be surer of their footing. However, Alicia was the same inquisitor as she had been on the ride up. She asked me about college, Chicago, my first girlfriend, my first kiss... she was endless and relentless.

The fog had pretty much burned off by the time we got back to the stables, so I was happy having the hat and sunglasses. I followed Alicia's lead, which turned out to include not only taking the saddles off and putting everything away, but also brushing down our horses.

I watched Alicia with Bronco and the way she talked to the horse. He seemed to listen. *The perfect 'girl and her horse' story....*

Alicia drove us back up to the house with her same attention to good driving techniques. When we got to my cottage, she surprised me by stopping the cart in front of it.

"Do you want out here or go all the way to the house?"

"Here will be good."

Before I could get out, Alicia added, "I had a good time. Maybe we could do this again tomorrow? We could try the beach this time."

Twelve going on twenty-two… she was asking for a 'second date.'

I smiled to myself. "Alicia, it was fun, and I would be happy to go on a beach ride with you tomorrow."

"Great. See you at dinner." She drove off.

I went inside my cottage. Took a shower and changed clothes. After that, I started working a bit. I had taken some of the paper files to my cottage yesterday with the thought I might be able to finish the first assignment before Monday morning. No one said I had to finish, but I thought it would make a good first impression.

Hey… I really have nothing else to do…Nothing except figure out if I am moving back to Chicago and starting a career as a corporate lawyer…

I was struggling a bit. That was obvious.

How am I going to figure all this stuff out?… Can I use the system Russ used with Kevin a couple of nights ago?

But that technique was for deciding between getting out of one thing and into something new. This was about two new things. Or was it? What really was the cost of leaving California and the benefits of going back to Chicago?

I started thinking and then remembered Russ had said if it was a big decision, take your time and go ahead and write the choices down. I opened my laptop up and started to put down the positives and negatives for California versus Chicago or Uncle Russ versus Don White and Fair Way Markets. I noticed two things were happening as I made the lists.

One, I felt less hopeless about the whole process. I felt proactive. It made me happy just knowing I was attacking the solution instead of hoping an answer would magically appear in my brain.

Two, this was truly a tough decision. There were good things and bad things on both lists… Things seemed to be leaning toward going back to Chicago. There was the money, the longer time horizon, being closer to my mother and more known aspects which all were adding up. But 'my adventure' had been really good in its first week – actually it was even less than a week… And then there was this issue with wondering what was 'behind the curtain' – Why me? Why now? – I wondered less about that now, but I still had no clue as to the answers.

Eventually, I realized it was time to go to dinner. It felt a bit odd to be thinking of leaving while I was still just getting acquainted with everything. I felt uncomfortable, so I decided I needed to speed the process up.

At breakfast, Anna had told me that in the kitchen in each cottage was a small clock display – a small box that looked like a clock radio with the time on it. It was not really the time. It was when dinner was being served that night. That way you didn't have to come up to the house or call to find out. I checked it and it said 7:00, so I decided being 15 minutes early this time would be good.

When I arrived at the house, Russ was in the kitchen helping Anna with barbequing the chicken and vegetables. I was still getting used to large indoor grills. I walked over. "Hi, can I help?"

"Hey Jay," Russ answered. "Sure, but first pour yourself some wine. I don't drink and Anna hates drinking alone, so making her feel better while she cooks would be a good start."

Anna gave him a small punch in the arm. "Jay, I'm doing fine. Just help yourself if you want to." I poured a glass and took a sip.

"We are running a bit late, so if you want to help, could you set the table.

"Sure."

"The plates are in the cupboard next to the freezer. The silverware is in the drawers below the cupboard, and the placemats are under the island. We only need nine tonight. Alex is staying at a friend's house."

Everyone else showed up just before seven, except for Alicia who was just a bit late, again. This time I ended up sitting between Kevin, who was next to Russ, and Alicia, who was next to Anna. The twins and their friends sat on the other side.

The conversation was mostly about what everyone did that day. The twins and Alicia and I went riding, Russ watched Alex's basketball team win their game by two points. Then Estelle asked what it was like to grow up where it snowed all winter. So I tried to describe Wisconsin winters as best as I could. Actually, snow is pretty neat when you're a kid. It gets more bothersome as an adult.

Then Russ said, "Since Alex is not here. Who is the next oldest for Word?" The four girls had a quick discussion and it turned out Charlotte, was five minutes younger than her twin sister. Charlotte thought for a second. Then, she looked directly at Russ and made her best effort to deliver a defiant face.

"Death."

Now there is a happy dinner word… I then saw a smile cross Russ's face.

"Excellent Charlotte. I was thinking on my next turn I would use that same word." He paused for a second then turned to Charlotte. "Is it okay if I expand it to 'Death, God and being happy'?"

Death, God and being happy… not three things I would have connected…

Charlotte was a bit surprised, but nodded 'yes'.

"Good." He paused again, then said, "I think death is probably the hardest topic any person ever thinks about. Most people avoid thinking about death and yet for me, the second most important word in our entire language is death." Everyone had now stopped eating. "Anyone care to guess the most important word?" He waited.

I was thinking as fast as I could. Then it came to me… *life…*

"Life?" I asked tentatively.

"Right Jay… Without life, there can be no death and without death, life would be pretty near meaningless. Let me explain that. If we all lived forever, nothing would happen. Just the opposite of what most people might think. If we didn't die, we would have no motivation to do anything at all. We wouldn't need to cook, eat, have children, or do anything. So, I suggest that the first thing we try to understand is that we will all die. And because of that fact, humans live the way we do."

Russ paused and I thought... *Boy that is about as direct as you can get. Sort of 'you will die, so get over it'....* I didn't realize how right I was.

"Okay, now that we have established that every one of us will die, what happens when we die?" No one said anything and no one was eating a bite. We were waiting for Russ to answer this question for us. "That's probably the toughest question you will ever have to think about... Thousands of books have been written on this question. Most religious books have sections on things like heaven and hell and what some call the afterlife."

"You mean like the Bible?" Kevin asked.

"Yes, the Bible is definitely one of those books." Russ continued, "That is where God comes in.... How many of you believe in God?"

Anna's hand went up first and soon everyone else's was up, including Russ who raised his last.

"Okay. People who believe there is no God, by definition, believe that when they die they will cease to exist in any way. Of course, they are only guessing there is no God. They have no real way to be sure."

"But since you all believe in God, we can continue down the path of what happens when we die." Russ paused again. "The question could thus be rephrased as 'What does God give us after death? Now comes the tricky and personal part. Until we die, we can't be sure. We can believe in something of course. We can believe in that something with every fiber in our bodies. But until we actually go through it, we will not know." Russ paused again.

I thought about it... *that is true...*

"So how do we deal with this question? Well you can get after-death ideas from movies or those thousands of books you may be reading. Or... you can just think on your own..."

I checked around the table and only Anna and Kevin were eating normally. The four teenage girls were all just listening without eating.

"In my case, I was raised as a Lutheran and went to church most Sundays when I was growing up. One thing that eventually helped me is a section of a book in the Bible called *Corinthians*. It basically says that as humans we cannot comprehend the afterlife God has in store for us."

"That simple idea saved me a lot of thinking time. I figured that if the Bible says that as a human I cannot comprehend what happens after death, then why should I spend any time thinking about it, because I will never find the answer."

"So my answer to the question of what happens after I die is not to think about it, as it's impossible to have a real answer."

"Now let's add the happy part."

Russ paused for a second and almost on cue all four girls picked up a piece of their chicken and took a bite.

"It turns out that that the minute you really accept that you will die one day, and that no matter how much thinking and believing you do, only God knows what happens next. At that moment, you will be free to stop worrying about dying. And once you stop worrying about dying, you can easily stop worrying about anything."

"And worrying is the number one reason people are not as happy as they should be."

"Unfortunately, my telling you this has little value for you by itself. You need to think about it on your own. Some people do so with religion. They believe with their whole heart in their religion's teachings on death, and that strong belief frees them from worrying about dying. Others just accept that only God knows and worrying about it is a waste of time."

Russ stopped and picked up a chicken leg and took a bite. Then he looked over at Charlotte with a big smile. "Charlotte, I hope this helps you think about life and death."

I don't know what Charlotte was expecting when she made death her Word... probably just a quick dismissal by GP... but definitely not this response... his answer on how to approach the toughest question a person can ever ask... Charlotte just nodded. She probably did not want to engage GP any further on this topic.

The twins and their friends were still quiet and trying to figure out whether they would eat more or... maybe they were just confused.

Kevin and Alicia... hmm I wonder what is running though those two heads... I'm sure they are processing this as best they can... And what about me... what am I thinking about here except for observing others? What is my personal process on death?

"Jay?" I woke up from my reverie.

"Jay? Can you pass the cookies?" Kevin was already moving on to dessert.

"Ah... sure." And I passed the cookie plate.

After I had finished dinner, I tried one of the chocolate chip cookies too. They really were good. Again, Russ asked if I wanted more berries and ice cream along with him. And again, I said 'yes'. The last couple of times I had chosen more berries and less ice cream, I noticed that Russ had mainly fruit . He asked me about my ride with Alicia and I told him how much fun it had been. And that Alicia had asked me for a Sunday ride.

He smiled. "Yes, she is very good at getting what she wants. I sometimes wonder if she isn't a bit too good at that for her own well-being." Then he asked me, "So what did you think of my death discussion for the kids?"

"Well, to be honest, I was captivated, so I'm not sure what they were thinking. When you got going, I was thinking I have never really spent much time on this topic."

"That is understandable. Nobody ever tells you to think about your own death as a way to be happy."

Russ looked up at the ceiling pensively and then back down. "I did most of my thinking about death in a two-week period when I was twenty-five. I was convinced I was smart enough to figure out the best answer. It was the most humbling experience of my life. I did most of that thinking while taking showers which must have lasted forever. I am not sure what my wife thought about it. I tried so hard, my head hurt and I even cried a couple of times at my failure to come up with a rational answer. But I couldn't."

"What I finally figured out, was that the answer for me was not to try to think of the answer. Just let God do what He was going to do anyway. Despite my upbringing, I'm not a very religious man, but I understand the concept of letting go of the most important issue in my life and know that when I die I will discover what God has in store for me… if anything."

He talked further as I took my last bite of berries and ice cream.

"I can tell you that once I did that, everything else became easy. If you're not worried about dying, you really aren't very worried about anything else. It allowed me to approach money… and success and failure with a take-it or leave-it attitude."

"If I could teach a class in how not to worry I would.' He paused for a second. "I watch too many people spend too much time worrying about the future. So, my goal would be to help people realize that if there is no reason to worry about dying, then why would you worry about money or friends or whatever? Compared to dying those issues are all pretty small."

He another took a bite of his dessert

Then I asked, "But how do you stop worrying about something that is going to happen in the future even if it is not death?"

"I am not sure that choice is as hard as it sounds. I think the key point is to understand the difference between 'planning' for the future and 'worrying' about it."

"It's okay, for example, to plan for retirement by saving money. But it's a waste of time to worry that it will not be enough to live the way you want to live when you retire. Worrying does not solve the problem. The solution is to either do what is necessary to save more now, or if that is not possible, then accept that your retirement will not be as you hoped and change your retirement plans to recognize reality. That way you can enjoy today and not be ruining it by worrying about tomorrow. Either do something or move on..."

Russ then took the last bite of his dessert.

Russ actually sounded a bit like my high school basketball coach only I knew this discussion was about real life. It was almost like he was 'willing me' to a happier life...

I could listen to him forever... Diana was right. He does have thoughts on everything. All you need to do is ask.

Diana... hmmm I wonder what she is up to... in Napa.

I decided to change the subject. "So Diana tells me she has been here almost two years and is going back to school."

"Yes, she's been great… I am still active in five of the ventures I helped start. And juggling them and getting the right information is really hard to do without someone like Diana to help me."

Maybe I can learn a bit more about her now… why do I have a slight tingling when I think about her…?

"How did you find her?"

"She found me. She is the daughter of one of my former partners who lives in Orange County. She wanted to have a job that would help her learn as much as possible before going to graduate school. Her Dad suggested this one. It has worked out great. She enjoyed it enough that she stayed an extra year and she was accepted at Stanford which was her first choice of schools."

Interesting, but not the personal information I was interested in.

"So she lives here and also in San Francisco?"

"Yes she rents a room up there from a friend of hers, so she has a place to stay in San Francisco whenever she needs it. You know it can be pretty boring down here for a twenty-four year old. But she sometimes brings friends down here as well. It's great fun for me."

Well, that was something to know. I think I need to drop this topic before Russ thinks I am really interested... am I really interested?

Then Russ said, "One game of air hockey?"

"Ah... sure."

We went to the game room and found the four girls bowling. I was amazed that I had not heard the noise of the pins in 'the kitchen'. The good news was that the game room was really big, and the air hockey game was as far away from the bowling as it could be, so I don't think we bothered them with our 'presence' too much.

I was a bit surprised to see the twins enjoying doing something together, but I guessed there must be a better bond than I thought earlier.

We ended up playing five games. I am happy to report that I won three of them. Also I figured out why Alex was so good. He must have been playing Russ for years, getting better as he grew bigger and practiced more.

After the games, we said good night. I went down to the cottage and starting writing in my journal again – there was a lot to write. Then it was off to bed. But my plan didn't work. I started to think about what Russ had said about death.

What does happen?

I never believed any of those 'I died and came back stories', so I was on my own here. Movies like *Ghost* came to mind, but they seemed to be too 'Hollywood Ending' to be worth contemplating seriously.

I had thought about death before, of course, but never with the idea of getting comfortable with actually dying someday. I always figured I was young and could deal with that problem later in life. But now those thoughts just kept coming at me.

What if God gives me nothing...? I mean nothing... like the second you die, no more thinking, no more you, forever...

A cold shiver went up my spine, and I felt even less like sleeping. I kept trying out different versions of what might happen, but none seemed to be more likely than any of the others. The last time I looked at the clock it read 2:00. Somehow I fell asleep after that. I was thinking this was a one-night experience... I was dead wrong.

8

I woke up to sunshine. It was going to be a beautiful day. The clock said 8:30, so I figured I had had at least six hours of sleep.

I decided to go right up the house and see if I could beat Alicia. I got ready quickly and walked up the path. The sun made everything look and feel different. The redwood trees were more majestic with the sunshine filtering through them. There were some wildflowers on the hill, and they looked bigger and brighter in the sun.

At the house I saw only Russ in the kitchen. He seemed hard at work. I opened the door, but he didn't appear to notice. Then I heard it.

I think he is singing… yes that is singing…

I didn't know what to do, so finally I just said, "Good morning, Russ." Seems my earlier decision to call him Uncle Russ had been short lived.

He turned around. "Hey, Jay. Didn't hear you come in."

Yeah, you were too busy singing…

"I'm making my famous omelets for breakfast this morning. Hope you will try one."

"Sure, what's in them?"

"That is the secret of my success. I have no idea what will be in them until I get down here and start cooking. I see what we have and then try to create the best tasting omelet I can think of from everything . I find it great fun."

"Certainly looks like you're having fun."

"I am. I love being creative, and omelet making is very creative for me. So I try to do it every Sunday."

"That's great." It was the only thing I could think to say. I had not made anything creative in a kitchen in a very long time... I am not sure I ever had.

"I think most people spend too much time doing things they either don't like to do or really do not care about and not nearly enough time doing something they truly enjoy. How can you be happy, if you don't spend your time doing the things that make you happy? So being a creative cook is one of my happy things."

"Today's version has diced Brussels sprouts, feta cheese, a little bit of chopped bacon, and some sautéed bean sprouts for texture. Are you hungry enough to try one?"

"Sure I would love one." I had no idea what it would taste like, but I was sure I would finish it even if I didn't like it.

Alicia walked in. "Hi GP, what are you making?"

"Omelets, Pumpkin. Want one?"

Pumpkin… that was new…

"Sure. Hi Jay. You want me to make lunch again today?"

"Ah… sure. Can I help?"

"No, I will be fine. I know where everything is."

Russ said. "I think I will join you two for breakfast. Kevin already ate, Anna is at church, and I think it's safe to say that four sixteen-year-old girls will not be down for breakfast for a good while. Who knows when they fell asleep."

Maybe before the 2 AM that I saw…

Alicia finished packing our lunches just as Russ finished the omelets, so we all sat down together.

Russ explained his day was waiting on the girls, taking them back to San Francisco and then picking up Alex. He had promised Alex burgers at the Dutch Goose near Stanford, so they would not be home for dinner. He also mentioned that Anna did not work on Sundays usually, so dinner was everyone finding leftovers from the week and picking what they wanted.

Alicia and I had a repeat day, except this one was all sunny and at the beach, near perfect weather in a near perfect location. She showed me a great view from the cliffs above the beach, and then we rode through some small waves. Finally, we had our picnic on a huge old tree trunk that had washed up and was resting in a small cove.

She asked me more about my 'ex-girlfriend' and somehow got me to tell her much of that story from meeting her to losing her. Alicia had a way of being totally interested in what you were saying, so much so you wanted to answer her questions right away.

I asked her if she had a boy she liked.

"I'm twelve. I have lots of time to do that."

Then she asked, "So you lost your one true friend and now you don't have one. Is that true?"

"My one true friend?"

"GP says everyone should try to have at least one true friend. A friend you can tell anything to and they will still like you and not abandon you no matter what you do. He always says that if you don't have one true friend, then get a dog. He says dogs can make great true friends when no human is there to be one. He said for five years his dog Z was his best friend."

She continued, "So I'm guessing Rachel was your one true friend and you lost her. Or is there someone else?

I thought about it for a minute, and she was right. I had no one.

"Yes, she was."

"That's okay. You'll find another one. GP says losing your one true friend hurts, but you will always find another one if you try. Right now my best friend is Bronco." She looked over at the horse who oddly seemed to understand he was being talked about. Bronco shook his head at her. "He is a good listener, never argues with me. Anyway, we don't have a dog, and there isn't one girl in my class right now that I can relate to that well."

The one true friend key... another lesson from Russ ... makes sense though... if you have someone you trust completely, it's easier to be happy than if you think you're all alone... interesting that a dog or horse qualifies... that must mean this is internal happiness... True Happiness...

Then I said, "Yes, it's good to have someone to talk to even if he or she can't talk back."

Alicia looked up and smiled at me.

After the ride and clean up in the stable, she drove us back like last time and dropped me off at the cottage.

"I think it's just you, me, Kevin and Anna for leftovers. We usually try to eat at six o'clock. Okay?"

"I will be there at six," I said and stepped out of the cart.

I went into my cottage, showered, changed clothes, and read a few more files. Again, I thought about Don White and the Fair Way offer. Or more precisely I thought about why I did not want to think about the offer.

I was afraid to think about it. I was afraid the offer would be too good to turn down. I did not want to quit the Farm, but… this offer could be my once-in-a-lifetime opportunity…

What I really wanted to do was ask Russ what I should do. But that was… impossible.

I went back to reading Russ's files and got far enough along that when it was time to head up to the house, I figured I had about an hour's work left before I would be finished. When I got to the house, Kevin, Alicia and Anna were busy getting the leftover containers out.

I noticed Kevin had earphones on from his IPod. I tapped him on the shoulder and he took one earphone out to hear me.

"What are you listening to?" I asked.

He looked at me with my intrusion. "Do know what French House music is?"

He was about to put his earphone back when I said, "Does Daft Punk wear helmets?" My favorite music was electronic music, and while I was no expert, I did pay attention to the genre.

I continued, "So what are you listening to?"

He smiled, handed me his IPod and earphones and said, "Here, you can listen if you want." My Daft Punk comment had gotten me a bit of recognition from Kevin.

He restarted the song and I put the earphones on. It was an excellent song, one I had not heard before. After it finished, I asked Kevin.

"Who is that?"

"Me."

I was not sure I heard him correctly. Maybe he misunderstood my question. Maybe he had taken someone's song and altered it???

"Ah... you did part of this song? Did you have a base song to work with?"

"No, it's an original song, I just made it up."

It was hard for me to believe that a nine-year-old could come up with a song this good on his own.

"Oh... sorry. Ah... how long did it take you to create it?" I was trying to recover.

"That song took a couple of days. Most of them take longer, but this one just seemed to invent itself.

"You have other songs?"

"Yeah, they're on the IPod. Want to listen?"

"Yes, I would, but I think first we should have dinner."

With just the four of us, the conversation was about normal stuff. No great Word game, just what was happening next week at school, etc.

After dinner, I sat with Kevin and he found the four other songs he had created. They were good, but only one other was as good as the first one I had heard.

I then had an idea. I asked Kevin if he could send me a copy of the songs. He seemed happy with the request and said he would.

While I was a novice in electronic music, one of my fraternity brothers from college was an expert. After graduation, he had helped create a group of online radio stations, and he was the electronic music lead for them. I was planning on sending the songs to him and asking him his opinion.

Soon it was back down to the cottage to finish my files.

When I opened up my computer, I noticed Kevin had already sent me the five song files. I picked the one I had first heard, listened to it again and then sent it and a note to my radio friend telling him that this kid I knew created this song and asking what he thought of it.

I then finished up the last of my files and headed to bed.

9

I woke up early for a change and saw it was another glorious sunny day.

This is really a special place. It's only my fifth day and I feel like I have landed in Camelot, where everyone is happy and nothing bad happens.

Boy - was I wrong.

I got dressed and headed up to the house by 8:00. I knew that Russ was a morning person, so I dropped the files on my desk and went into his office to see if he was there yet.

"Hi Jay. Close the door and come sit over here." There were two stuffed chairs next to the floor to ceiling windows with a table in between them… a great view on a clear day. Russ was sitting in one of the chairs. I sat down in the other one. There was an open Diet Coke on his side of the table.

"I'll come right to the point." He paused for a second and then said, "The reason you're here to help is that I am dying"

What??? Dying???Did he say he was dying?

"Dying?" I said the word more as a reflex reaction than actually thinking about what it meant.

"Yes. It's a long story, but the short version is I have a bad pancreas… more specifically inoperable, acute, chronic, idiopathic pancreatitis. It has been in remission for almost twenty years. It came back about a month ago. I went to Stanford Hospital, and they confirmed it. Their best guess is I have six months to a year to live. It could be less, could be more. With a miracle, it goes back in remission, but they don't think so."

He is really dying… He doesn't act like he's dying…

"At this point, I've only told Lynn. So you're the second person. I do not like holding back, but there are a few things I would like to take care of first. And the thought of a year of sad goodbyes seems awful painful to me."

Okay… I get it… who is Lynn?

"I have left a lot of my business paperwork in less than, shall we say, a 'pristine' condition. So with your help and that of my regular lawyers, I'm hoping to get it all straightened out while I'm still here to explain everything."

So this is why I am really here… I guess it really isn't something you just say on the phone…

"Ah… I see. Okay." It was all I could think to say. If I said I was sorry he was dying, I would be doing just what he didn't want anyone to do.

"I've decided in the short run to tell my business partners that I'm planning a yearlong sabbatical, and I want to make adjustments accordingly. That is partially true. Lynn and I are planning a two-month trip to start in May. After that, I will probably not want to spend too much time on business, so the effect is the same."

My thoughts bounced around some more… *I see he has logically thought this through… Who is Lynn? … Russ is really dying… I just met him, and already I feel bad that I will be losing him….*

"I think the best thing to do is go through each of the investments or operating companies and discuss the best plan for each. Any questions?"

Yeah, about a million actually… But the only one I could think of to say out loud was an obvious one.

"So you're really sure this is happening? I mean, you seem so healthy and normal… so I ….."

"I understand," he answered. "I feel perfectly healthy right now. But what's going to happen is that the pancreatic attacks will get stronger and stronger. What the doctors have told me is that either I'll have one or two massive attacks which will stop most things in my body, or over time the attacks will cause serious damage to the organs around the pancreas, and I will die of the complications that damage causes. In the meantime, when I get mild attacks, I can just use painkillers to get over them. There is no fixing this situation, unfortunately."

That doesn't sound very good...

Russ continued, "I have found in my life that I do much better if I accept a new reality when I can't change it. The quicker I adjust, the better able I am to deal with it and make the best decisions for me. Also, the quicker I get back to enjoying my life as it is. I do have to admit this new reality has been hard to accept. I'm the most sad that I will not be there to watch my grandchildren grow up. That and not growing old with Lynn are the two things that are the worse things."

I guess he thinks I must know who Lynn is... I will ask Diana when I see her...

"So let's get started on a quick review. It shouldn't take too long. Maybe we can get it done today. I've scheduled us for a meeting with the lawyers tomorrow morning in Mountain View."

With that he started in on a discussion of all his business ventures.

After about an hour, Russ paused and looked up.

"Jay, I just want to say that I'm sorry that I have put a bit of my burden on you. I hope you don't let it get in the way of enjoying your time here on the Farm and interacting with the grandkids. I've noticed that Alex, Alicia and Keven have already warmed up to you, and that is great."

"Yes," I said. "They are three great kids." But, I was really thinking - *How could this not dampen everything*? I didn't know it then, but Russ would soon teach me how.

Russ continued on, "My plan is to try to accomplish three things in the next months. Give as many lessons to the grandkids as possible, spend some good quality time with Lynn, and get these businesses straightened out. I owe it to my partners to try and do that.

With that we dug back into the files. I was so totally focused on taking notes and trying to understand everything Russ wanted that I did not hear the knock at the door.

But Russ did. "Come in."

It was Diana. She had just returned. With all the news and focus on business, I had completely forgotten she would be back around lunch time.

She said she was hungry and wondered if we had eaten lunch yet. Russ answered that we hadn't and a lunch break sounded like a great idea.

Russ chatted with Diana as we walked down the hall, asking about her weekend and her time in Napa, I was struck for the first time by the enormity of what Russ had told me.

This changes everything... and Lynn and I are the only ones who know right?... who is Lynn? Can't be his mother, he wouldn't call her Lynn.

Anna had taken the kids to school in the morning and was still out. Thus, lunch was 'make your own sandwiches' or leftovers. I decided to heat up some spaghetti, and it was really good.

I looked out the window at the stunning view of the Pacific Ocean and thought more about the news Russ had given me earlier. It was the second time in three months I had received sudden tragic personal news. I was again struck by how everything else in the world seemed unaffected. The sun shone on a wonderful day. The waves crashed on the beach as they had been doing for millions of years. Anna was out shopping for food, and the kids were at school. Everything just moved along as if nothing had happened. But inside my brain, I heard a scream of emotional pain. This man who had somehow decided to 'rescue' me from my depressed state was in fact dying and dying fairly quickly.

Our lunch conversation was a combination of business and personal items. Russ told Diana that he and I would be in Mountain View tomorrow morning and so she should handle the Paris operations conference call.

"I think you understand the Google SEO process better than I do. That is the main point of tomorrow's call. So go ahead. I think you will do great."

"I'm not as sure about that, but Pierre, Bertrand, and Thomas are very easy to work with, sort of French gentlemen."

Russ laughed, "That may be true of Pierre. I think Bertrand and Thomas are still in their twenties, so it's good there is an ocean between you and them."

I had read the file on the Paris travel company. Pierre was the original partner, and Bertrand and Thomas were the two who were running most of the company's marketing and operations. This was one of the more active projects that Russ was working on.

"And," Russ continued, "They are very pleased with the AdWords campaigns you've been designing for them, so they may be more willing to listen to your next project idea."

We finished lunch and put away the dishes and extra food.

Russ said, "Jay. There is always time for an air hockey game or two. You up for it? I'm feeling 'it' today."

"Ah… sure." We headed off to the game room.

"Well, someone has to work," Diana called out with a smile and she headed up the stairs to her office.

Russ laughed. "Work is highly overrated, my dear."

As we entered the game room, Russ added his thoughts. "Too many people work too hard and play too little. If you calculate the amount of time they spend at their jobs, commuting, working at home, working on their houses or cars or running errands, they have very little time left for fun. Then most of them just watch TV. At least TV is not work, but it is a brain damper with almost no real fun. At least that is what it is for me."

"Remember to add real fun to every day. That said, it's your serve, Jay."

After our air hockey time where he beat me this time, we went back to Russ's office to finish up on the files. Even though I was trying to focus on the work, my mind kept having other thoughts.

What would I be doing if I had a year or less to live? ... Russ seems totally at ease... I wonder if it's his attitude towards death he said the other night? ... I guess if you really are 'comfortable' with dying, then this is how you'd act with a year left... just enjoying life.

The progress was quick on the files. We decided to keep pushing through and finished just in time for dinner. I ended up at the front of the dinner line, and shortly after I sat down, Alicia sat on one side of me and Kevin on the other. Both had things they wanted to talk about.

Alicia told me that Wednesdays were half days at school so she would be home by one and could I go riding with her? It was only Monday, but I could see her plotting ahead already.

"I might have to..." I started to answer as I was sure that I would have work to do. But Russ was listening and gave me a small nod of approval. "I would love to," I responded

Kevin said he had spent the afternoon creating a new song and wondered if after dinner I could listen to it and give him my thoughts. I said 'yes' to that request too.

Diana was seated across from me. I saw her smile as she saw me getting 'waylaid' by the kids. She also seemed 'pleased' by the way the kids were interacting with me. For some reason, I was pleased that she was pleased with me...

It turned out to be Diana's night for 'the Word'. So when it came time to start the 'game', she asked, "How do you decide what to do in life?"

Wow... that is a tough question... can't wait to see how Russ tries to handle this one.

I didn't have to wait too long as Russ launched in.

"Big question, Miss Diana." He paused a bit, a continued.

"I got this all wrong when I was your age. I looked at what other people did and looked at what made other people happy. And I listened to what other people thought I would be happy doing. My father so much wanted me to become a Wall Street lawyer. I even applied to law school. It was a good thing I got turned down by the schools I wanted to go to, or I might have done that.

So let me approach it this way. One question to ask might be 'what do you want your life to be about?' and another is 'what career and life choice do I want to make? Do you think that is a decent start?'"

"I guess so… sure" Diana hesitated with her answer. I think it was because she wasn't sure she understood what Russ had just said.

"So Diana, I think twenty-four is a good age to ask these kinds of questions. Even younger is okay." He looked all the grandkids in the eye as he continued.

"Many people's lives are about helping others. From waiting tables in a restaurant, to being funny to make people laugh, to going into medicine to help them stay healthy, to writing poetry to get them to think, to going into non-profit work to help right wrongs, to joining the police, fire, and the

Army to keep people safe, to being a good parent to help raise happy children, to working in a Hawaiian resort to help people have better vacations, even to making cars to help people move around better.

So you can see, it's a pretty wide open field for ways your life can be about helping others." He paused to see if the kids were still following him.

"It's true that some people pick more selfish goals like more money, bigger houses, fancier parties, cooler clothes and cooler friends. But I suggest we skip over those goals, as you can probably agree they are pretty hollow, egotistical goals which in the end do not bring lasting happiness – at least from my experience.

Now, of course you can have more than one of these goals at the same time, say raising great children and saving lives as a fireman. As your life changes over time, you will probably change some of what you want your life to be about."

"I don't get it," Alicia blurted out. "What does all of that mean?"

I admit, Russ was going quickly and I wasn't sure what it was all about either.

Russ looked at Alicia. "I'm sorry to be going too fast. What I was trying to say is that when you're trying to decide what your life is going to be about, there are lots of things to pick from, and most relate to helping others… or making them happy. When I gave all those examples, maybe I confused you."

"Yeah," Alicia said. "So if I get this, when I think about my life and what I want to do with it, I'm probably thinking about some way I can help others. Right?"

"Yes… I think most people do that whether they do it on purpose or not. As I said, there are some people who only think of themselves. My thought here is that those people are unlikely ever to really be happy as they fall into the trap of trying to get external 'stuff' to give themselves internal happiness. It doesn't work very well."

"Got it," Alicia said quickly.

"So this leaves the problem of how do you relate what I'm saying to the decision of what you want to do with your life. That is indeed a much tougher question."

I had wanted to be a lawyer for so long that I no longer really remembered why I wanted to be one. I just sort of became one.

Russ continued, "So first you have to give an honest assessment of yourself. For example, you may envision yourself entertaining the world as a great singer, when in fact you have a limited singing voice. No amount of determination and practice will change that circumstance. The decision of what to do in your life has to blend your personal goals with your reality. It sounds a bit like a psychology text book, but in real life it is much simpler."

Alicia interrupted again. "GP, what has your life been about?"

Russ laughed. "Alicia, I can always count on you to ask the 'tough' questions."

"When I was your age, I either wanted to be an Air Force pilot because I loved the jet fighters I saw in the movies and the plastic jet models in the hobby shop… or a professional basketball player. I would shoot baskets in my driveway all the time even in the snow. I would pretend to be Jerry West from the Lakers and hit game winning shots."

"Then when I got to be Alex's age, I dropped the Air Force pilot idea and decided I just wanted to be rich. I didn't really care how that happened. I just made it a goal. I also lost the professional basketball player dream when I noticed that other guys on the team were faster than me… I could see I wasn't going to be good enough."

"That lasted until I met your grandmother while we were in college. Then I added being a great friend and husband to Margie to what I was going to do. I still kept 'wanting to be rich'." Russ laughed a bit.

"I had figured out that the only way for me to be rich was to do well in business. My father's route for me was to have me become a big time lawyer on Wall Street. But I couldn't get into the schools I needed to do that. But, I had studied hard though and after working for a couple of years, I was accepted into the Stanford Business School. I figured it was a great first step to becoming rich. But instead, I met some of the alumni who had started companies and I felt the passion they felt for their efforts. Soon I found myself wanting to be creative and help start a company more than I wanted to be just rich. Rich became something that might happen or might not happen."

"Then two major things occurred that gave me the definition I needed for the rest of my life."

"First, I was in a position to hire people to work at a company that I had started with a friend. There was something about the smile on their faces and the upbeat sound of their voices when I told them we wanted to hire them that I found totally rewarding. I learned I was able to combine my creativity and passion for starting companies with the joy of giving people jobs. That became my lifelong focus."

"The second event was the birth of your Uncle Mark. I went from not thinking twice about children to wanting to give my children the best childhood as they grew up… When your cousin Dan was born, I added grandchildren to that list…" Russ paused and looked at the kids. "How am I doing?"

Alicia answered without skipping a beat. "Pretty good… so far. Still, I think less chores and more desserts for grandchildren would put you over the top."

"Nice try young lady," was Russ's response.

It was a lively discussion after that with everyone asking more and more questions about Russ and his time growing up.

At the end of dinner, Russ offered a recap of the upcoming week. "I just want to make sure everyone knows the schedule going forward for this weekend. Lynn will be here Friday night, and Saturday, we have an 11 AM flight to Maui. We will be back the next Thursday night. Alex, Alicia and Kevin, you're scheduled to have weekend sleepovers at friends. If anything goes wrong, your Uncle Mark will pick you up, and you'll spend the weekend there. Anna will be flying to Los Angeles to see Manny and will come back Monday morning and pick the three of you on Monday afternoon from school. Any problems, call Diana. Jay and Diana, I will have projects for you to do next week which don't need me so that schedule should work well."

"Any questions…" Russ paused. "If not, Anna has a double fudge chocolate cake ready for us, and I suggest you cover it with ice cream…" The kids stormed the kitchen where they waited for Anna to come and cut the cake.

I was slow to finish my dinner and then even slower to finish my cake when I found myself at the table with only Diana sitting across the table from me.

"I see you have been charming the kids?" she said with a smile.

"It's more like they have charmed me." I answered. "I'm surprised at how perceptive they are, especially Alicia."

"Yep, she seems to have you wrapped around her little finger."

"Ah… yes." I admitted. "I do find it hard to say 'no' to her."

Then the question I had wanted to ask all day popped into my head. "Who is Lynn?"

"Lynn?" Diana did not seem to understand the question. Then her eyes widened. "Oh, Lynn. Her Name is Lynn Baldacci. She is Russ's girlfriend. Has been for I think at least ten years."

"I was thinking it was something like that given the whole Hawaii discussion." Diana continued.

"Lynn is usually here about half the time. She runs a public relations firm in San Francisco and has a house there. She and Russ are as good as married… except they're not. Russ told me he asked several times, but that Lynn said she didn't want to be married. She likes her job too much and loves living in The City too much to want to have a different relationship from the one they have. I think you will like her when you meet her. Everyone does. She has one of those personalities that is smart and sophisticated and yet warm and caring… and when she talks to you, you feel you are the only person in the world she wants to listen to."

"Wow… sounds like you're chairman of her fan club."

Diana laughed. "Yep. Pretty much. I think she is great and if I grow up to be like her, I will be very happy." She paused and then said, "Have you ever spent much time in San Francisco?"

"No. I drove through on the freeway last week and that is my entire experience with it."

"Do you want to come to San Francisco this weekend with me?"

With her? … Did I hear her right? …

Diana continued quickly, "I'm going up Saturday morning, and if you don't mind sleeping on our couch, I think my roommate would be okay with you coming along. I could show you some highlights and on Saturday night, we are meeting a bunch of friends in the Marina. I think you might have fun."

"That sounds great."

She just invited me to join her in San Francisco...
where did that come from? ...

"Good, I plan to leave by nine. Hope that's not too early?"

I smiled, "No. I've gotten used to how quiet it is here. I am waking up at a decent hour now."

Alex had come back in the kitchen and yelled over to me, "How about one game of air hockey?"

Diana smiled at me and softly said one word, "Charmed."

"Sure Alex. I'll meet you in the game room."

I put my dishes in the dishwasher and told Diana, "Thanks for the invitation."

"No problem"

I headed down the hall to the game room. Alex beat me four straight and was encouraging me to focus more on my defense as he headed to his room and I went down to my cottage.

I started reading my Dick Francis book. I also thought about everything that had happened...

This morning I woke up thinking I was in Camelot. And now the main person making Camelot what it is, is dying... and I'm going to San Francisco with Diana this weekend... things change quickly around here....I wonder if that has always been true, but I never noticed it before... too busy focused on my life plan and not life itself...

There was a ping on my laptop. The sound of a new email coming in. I knew instinctively it was the offer email from Don White.

What am I going to do?... I can't leave Russ now... This may be my only chance to really know this fascinating relative of mine... And, I can't pass on the Fair Way offer either. It would be stupid.

Then Diana's question at dinner came back. Maybe Uncle Russ was giving me the advice I needed to make a decision. *What do I want my life to be about?*

I fell asleep thinking about that...

10

Tuesday was a long work day. Russ drove us over the hill into the Silicon Valley and into Mountain View. Driving through Palo Alto and Mountain View was somewhat historic for me. I had grown up as a digital generation kid. Here were so many famous consumer tech names here, companies either started or now had headquarters like; Google, Yahoo, Apple, Facebook, You Tube, and PayPal.

We met with the lawyers at Fenwick & West who worked on Russ's account. The partner, Matt Lawson, was especially nice.

We did not finish until after 6 PM. As we were driving back, Russ announced, "Let me show you the Stanford Campus."

And so he did, complete with a bit of history and his theory on how Stanford got to be as well regarded as it was.

The campus itself is much different than most. It's on a huge piece of property that was deeded to the school in the 1800's. The property is so big that besides the main education campus and all the sports stadiums and the hospital complex and the largest shopping mall in the San Francisco

Bay Area, it also has three small lakes, a cattle ranch, and a large office complex with dozens of large office and high tech buildings, including the headquarters of Hewlett Packard and Tesla Motors. In the back area there was still room for an almost two-mile long linear accelerator building.

Just as we were leaving campus, Russ suggested we have dinner at an old restaurant called Buck's in Woodside, a town near the campus. He told me Buck's was one of a kind, and when we walked in, I understood why. There were crazy memorabilia and odd items everywhere.

Right over our head was a full size, high tech, motor-less racer. I asked what it was, and Russ explained that at one time some venture capitalists had established a charity race for motor-less vehicles. And being the competitive types they were, they spent way too much time and money trying to win the race. The racer above us was supposedly tested in the NASA wind tunnel at Moffett Air Force Base.

I ordered my favorite dish, a Cobb salad, and Russ went with a burger and fries.

"I used to meet people here all the time when I lived on this side of the hill. I always liked watching how they dealt with the overload of things hanging on the walls and ceiling. I noticed I seemed to like those people who stopped working long enough to check the stuff out and ask questions. I think it was their ability to step back and enjoy life that drew me to them."

Then he asked me, "How are you feeling these days? Your mom said you took the break-up with your fiancée pretty hard."

Where did that question come from? ...

"I'm not trying to pry, but I have had a number of personal losses in my life, so I was thinking I could maybe relate."

So I answered, "I certainly feel better here after a week than I have the last couple of months. I think all the newness has helped me to stop focusing on how it. That said, when I do think about it, it still hurts pretty deeply."

Russ looked straight at me as I spoke. He had those kind of understanding eyes that made you feel comfortable. "My second wife left me. I was so in love with her at the time. I think she was just bored with me, I'm not really sure. But it was then I discovered a good way to deal with the bad things that always seem to happen in your life."

As Diana said, he has a thought on every topic...

"I call it, Forgive, Forget, Move On. Maybe it sounds familiar, but my version is a bit different."

"First, I try to forgive myself or the other person or both, depending on the circumstance. I have found it's easier for me to forgive myself than the other person."

I have definitely not forgiven Rachel...

"Whether or not I'm able to forgive, I go immediately to forget. I find it is mainly based on time although as you have probably noticed, if you have other things to occupy your brain, then forgetting happens faster."

Forgetting is happening only when I'm busy...

"But most importantly, I 'move on'. And I don't wait for forgive and forget to happen. I move on right away. I think we talked about accepting reality. It is the key to moving on. You look at the facts as they are, not as you wish they were. Then you figure out the best path toward getting back your happiness, and you 'move on'."

That may be the key. Is Diana part of my 'move on'?

I didn't say anything, and after a pause Russ added, "Anyway, this works for me."

"No, No." I guess my face showed some disbelief. "I was thinking this was exactly what I needed right now. A way to get past everything. Move on as you say."

We continued on with our conversation, some work stuff, and basically anything I asked about. Russ knew what was happening in Syria and Malaysia and China as well as the injuries to the Boston Celtics and how it might affect the NBA playoffs. It was fun just talking with him, bring up new topics, and listen to what he knew about them.

Then I remembered, *He's dying… and there is nothing anyone can do about it.*

I felt a stab of sadness. But if Russ noticed, he just kept talking through it, and I got past it quickly.

We got home late and I went straight to my cottage.

I reread the offer letter from Don White. It was a good offer. I figured that if the Fair Way IPO happened as anticipated the stock options they offered would be worth over $1 million. Of course, I would have to work there for four years to earn them all, but if the company did well, it was possible the stock could be worth more than $2 million by then.

I looked at the California versus Chicago lists again.

The biggest negative wasn't the four years. It was that I would be back working with my old boss. I would be the client this time, but I was sure there would be tension. Maybe lots of it. I certainly wasn't past all the betrayal. And then, there would be my 'betrayal' of Uncle Russ…

Just thinking about everything got my emotions riled up again. It took me an hour to calm down and fall asleep.

11

The next day Russ and I were going over the comments that Fenwick & West had made and were working away when Alicia popped in.

"You ready?"

I turned around, and for a second I forgot that I had committed to taking another ride with her.

Russ answered for me. "Good time to take a break. Have fun and I'll see you tomorrow morning

Alicia and I headed down to one of the golf carts. Alicia said she had packed us a snack.

I was getting used to Alicia's driving and found myself not hanging on in the curves. I knew she would not take them too fast. She talked quite a bit about school and the ups and downs of her week so far. I asked how Kevin was doing.

"The same. Basically no real friends. Only a couple kids interact with him. I think his decision to drop baseball was a good one. Those 'friends' were not really all that nice to him either."

Bronco was once again excited to see Alicia. They did a few rounds in the jumping arena, and then Alicia said she would show me Dragon Lake. The ride there was fun. I was feeling more comfortable, so we ran the horses a bit on a couple of the flat fields.

Dragon Lake turned out to have a more mysterious name than reality. It was a small tree-lined lake about ten acres in size. It was quite pretty as one edge had a nice view of the coastline. The name came from a large old oak tree that had the shape of dragon as you approached. Nothing more sinister than that I thought.

Again, Alicia knew a good picnic spot on the edge of the lake and once there she got out our snack.

"So you kind of like Diana, right?"

I paused and gave her an odd glance.

Where does she get this stuff from?

She then answered her own question. Sort of. "I see the way you look at her, and I was guessing that is how you look when you like someone… you know what I mean."

Alicia was so straight forward. I wanted to answer the same way.

"Yes, I know what you mean. And to answer your question, I'm not sure. I'm still getting over Rachel, so I'm uncertain about how I feel about anyone. That said, I do find Diana a very nice person to be around."

"Oh." That was all she said, but then after a long pause, she added. "I was just going to tell you that I think she likes you too. I mean I see her looking at you when she knows you are not looking at her... seems to me she's interested."

Wow! Nothing gets past this girl... I thought I had noticed a look from Diana... this confirms it...

"Aren't you the little matchmaker." It was a weak response, but it was all I could think of to turn our talk back to being about her and not me.

She just smiled and took another bite of her apple. After a little bit she asked, "Do you like to fish?"

"Not really," I answered. "I do not have the patience to enjoy it."

"Oh... GP stocked this lake a few years ago, and the fish have acclimated. There are lots to catch if you want to try some time."

"Do you like to fish?" I asked back.

"No, I don't like to bait the hook. And GP says if you're going to fish. you have to do all your own work. You know, bait the hook, catch the fish, and then take it off the hook so you can put it back. I only like the catching part."

I laughed, "At least you know what you want."

We rode back, did a couple more races. I enjoyed watching Alicia and Bronco interact. She talked to that horse almost non-stop.

I was starting to have a twelve-year-old friend I could actually talk to. It seemed easier for me to talk with Alicia than Diana or even Russ.

Wonder why that is? ...

That afternoon I called Don White with my decision. I told him 'no'. I told him it was the great offer that he had promised, but at this point I was not ready to make a jump into the world of corporate lawyer.

What I really had decided was that I was going to follow Russ's lessons. I was going to Forgive (myself), Forget (as best as I could), but definitely Move On (from any connection with my past in Chicago). I was going to enjoy My Adventure here with my 'Uncle' Russ (and Alicia, Kevin, Alex, Diana and Anna) and not worry where it was leading right now.

After the call, I felt relieved... and also a bit scared. I had just turned down what might be the best career offer I was ever going to get in my life...

12

The next two days were pretty simple. I worked with Russ and the Fenwick & West lawyers, played with the kids, and pretty much enjoyed myself.

Friday evening arrived and with it Lynn's appearance at the Farm. Apparently her 'status' at the Farm was such that she just parked her car out front and walked in the front door, as the first thing I knew she was in the house and standing in my office doorway introducing herself.

"Hi. I'm Lynn. You're Jay. Correct?" Her voice was calm and friendly. I looked up and Russ's girlfriend was walking toward me with her hand stretched out to shake mine.

She continued, "Russ has said so much about you this past week. It's nice to meet you in person."

I stood up quickly and came around my desk to shake her hand. "Nice to meet you too."

Lynn was tall with sophisticated short hair and a very pretty face. She was dressed in what I guessed was San Francisco female executive attire, a very fashionable black skirt, nice white top with top buttons not buttoned and a tight cut black jacket over it. She was wearing black heels which could have been Jimmy Choo's (if I knew what a Jimmy Choo shoe looked like). She looked to be in her early forties. I found out later she was fifty-two.

She turned, closed my door and sat down. "We might not have an opportunity to talk privately later, so I thought I would ask you how Russ is doing. Have you noticed any attacks?"

Attacks?... Oh pancreatic attacks...

"Ah... no, I haven't noticed anything. But I'm not with him all the time."

"That's okay. The doctors told me one way of gauging the progression of the disease was the frequency of attacks. The fact you've been spending long periods with him and haven't noticed anything is good news... very good news. I have been on a business trip the last ten days and am relieved to hear nothing has changed."

I realized now why she had come to see me first. I was the only one she could ask these questions to.

She seemed to relax quite a bit at this point. "I'm sorry to push so hard. We've just met. But I have been so worried these past days. I knew that Russ would not tell me, so I didn't even bother to ask him." She paused and looked around my office. It was strewn with files everywhere.

"Looks like you've been here a month. Is everything going okay? I know Russ will feel better when he straightens this stuff up."

She seems to know everything... Then I thought. *I wonder what 'everything' includes... my guess is that everything means everything...including everything about me...*

"I think we have made a bunch of progress. Fenwick & West is already working on most of the investment documents."

"Good to know. Russ said you have been very helpful even in your first week." She smiled and looked me in the eye. "And he also said Alicia had you 'wrapped around her little finger' already. I think that is good for her. She and Kevin are very bright, and that can be hard on them socially."

"I know. Alicia already told me about Kevin, but I also sensed to some degree she was also talking about herself... I have a great time riding with her. She opens up even more when she is riding."

"Yes." Lynn answered. "She loves her horse more than anything else in this world. I think it helps her to have him. As Russ says, 'her one true friend'."

Everyone here speaks in Russ-isms...

We talked a few more minutes with Lynn asking about my mother and how I was enjoying the Farm. Then she noted, "You know. The best thing you can do for Russ is really enjoy your time here at the Farm. He built it for people to enjoy. and it makes him feel good when he sees people doing that."

"I'm enjoying it very much actually."

"Great." She stood up. "I'd better track him down before he thinks I'm conspiring against him. Which I guess is exactly what I'm doing…"

She laughed. "See you at dinner." With that she was out the door.

Before meeting Lynn, I had no idea what kind of woman would be attractive to Russ and vice versa. Now that I had met her, I understood completely. She was strong without being controlling. She had a warm and funny side to her and yet she apparently was running a successful PR firm in San Francisco which would mean she could compete and deliver. Just the personality combination it would take to keep Russ interested and just the kind of person who could put up with his all-encompassing personality/ego without feeling in the least bit intimidated.

I doubt Lynn ever feels intimidated…about anything…

I heard Russ greet Lynn as she entered his office. "Hey Babe." She laughed, and I heard the door close...

After finishing a couple more files, I went down to my cottage to change for dinner. I guess I thought I needed to show a better side of me than what I had been wearing when I met Lynn. I could tell she was already 'up-scaling' me...

Dinner was an adult affair this time, as the kids were at their friends for the weekend. When I got to the kitchen, Anna asked me how I liked my steak cooked. She said that since Russ and Lynn were heading to Hawaii, she wanted to make something they were not likely to order there.

Right before dinner, she put out some deviled eggs. I'm 'addicted' to deviled eggs. I had to make sure I didn't eat too many.

Lynn poured some wine, and Russ poured diet coke in a wine glass, which he explained made it feel more like a party to him than just having a can or a regular glass with it.

He does know how to keep fun in the front of his brain...

The steaks were fabulous. With baked potatoes, Brussels sprouts and creamed spinach. I could not think of a better Friday night dinner.

The conversation was wide ranging, from politics in San Francisco, to Anna's son Manny, (she was flying to see him in the morning), to what to do in Maui, to my growing up in Wisconsin. Lynn asked the most questions and she clearly focused on the answers and followed them up with more questions.

Lynn and Russ doted on each other, with arm snuggles and quick kisses on the cheek whenever one of them said something 'endearing' about the other. Lynn's eyes often simply stared at Russ's face as he told a story.

At one point I asked how they had met. They both laughed.

It turned out that Lynn had made a business pitch to one of the companies that Russ had invested in. Russ was in the meeting by accident, as he was meeting with the company's Marketing VP, who had casually asked Russ to join him.

As Lynn told it, "My pitch failed to impress the VP, but Russ caught me in the hall and asked me to dinner. I was all set to say 'no' when he put that 'poor puppy dog' look on his face and made me feel sorry for him. I was not happy I did not get the account. But Russ has said since that if I had been hired, he might not have asked me out, as it might have been looked 'unprofessional' – as if that has ever stopped him... Well... we've been together ever since."

uss pitched in, "After making a bunch of mistakes, I finally realized that first you figure out where you are going with your life and then you find the person who will go with you. I kept getting it in the wrong order. And if you get that wrong, it can be very painful for a very long time. I have the 'scars' to prove it."

Anna also chimed in which she rarely did. "That is exactly what I keep telling Manny. All these girls just want to get married and have kids."

"He needs one that has the same goals he does. He wants to be a chef, and that means moving a few times as he learns his skills and gets a restaurant of his own. It could take five to ten years and several moves. So he should either find a girl who is good with that or wait to find a girl after he gets his restaurant. I don't know if he listens though…"

I started to think… *What did Rachel really want?… I don't think I ever asked… that seems pretty stupid now…*

We finished the night with, you guessed it, berries and ice cream. But this time everyone was sitting around the fireplace. Lynn was curled in on Russ. As she talked, she kept putting her hand on his hand or his leg and then squeezed it gently when she made a point. It was very endearing to watch.

The whole evening had a very nice family feeling. I kept looking over at Diana, and a couple of times I actually 'caught' her looking at me. She just smiled when that happened.

Tomorrow should be very interesting...

Boy did that turn out to be an understatement...

13

Saturday morning was hectic. Anna was busy making sure Russ and Lynn were ready. Of course she had packed for herself the night before. The plan was for her to go with them to the airport and park the car. When she came back on Monday, she would just use the same car to get the kids at school.

I woke up early and packed an overnight bag – basically a change of clothes and my toothbrush.

I admit I was getting a bit nervous about spending a whole weekend with Diana. I tried to read my Dick Francis novel, but I could not focus. Finally, at 8:30, I went up to the house. Anna was in the kitchen when I let myself in.

"Hi Anna. All set for LA?"

"Yes, packed and ready to go... I'm making French toast. Would you like some?"

"Great."

"How many slices?"

"How big are they?" I was learning…

"Texas size."

"Then two will be plenty."

I was getting juice when Lynn and Russ appeared. Anna asked them about French toast, and they hesitated. Then they said the food was terrible on airplanes, so 'yes' they needed some.

Anna smiled... I saw she liked 'making a sale'.

We talked about their favorite spots in Maui. It seemed they went to Hawaii for at least a week every year.

'Remember to have fun'... that is what he told me and I can see he really lives it...

They had a favorite place in Maui - Kapalua, a favorite restaurant – Sansei Sushi, a favorite hiking trail – the abandoned Kapalua Village mountainside golf course trail, even a favorite breakfast place – the Sea House, apparently an untouched diner from Hawaii circa 1960 that was located literally on the sand.

It was obvious they were looking forward to this trip a lot. But I kept thinking. *Is this their last visit to Maui?...* I couldn't help myself.

They were all excited about what they were going to do. I wondered how they could just do that. Then, I remembered what Russ had said a couple of days ago.

Don't let something from your past or in your future ruin your today... and this is what they were doing... this was maybe their last trip to Maui, but they were not letting that fact ruin their trip.

I watched them more closely and their genuine excitement... *amazing and wonderful...* was all I could think.

At five minutes to nine, Diana showed up. She looked spectacular. I was surprised at how pretty she was. I wasn't sure why, but I guess during the week she didn't take the extra time to fix her hair as much. Or maybe it was the cool outfit she had on. Whatever it was that was different... I was impressed.

"Good morning everyone," she announced as she came down the stairs.

"French toast?" Anna asked.

"No thanks, Anna. I'm just going to eat a banana this morning... Are you all excited about your trips?"

Lynn, Russ and Anna started talking all at once about how much they were looking forward to Maui and Los Angeles.

Then Diana looked at me and said. "And you, Mr. Knight, are you looking forward to our grand tour of San Francisco?"

I thought... *Excited... and nervous....*

But I said, "Absolutely. I love having my own personal tour guide."

"Okay then, I think we can be off."

We said our goodbyes and went out the front door where Diana had parked her Mini. She had told me earlier that a Mini improved her odds of finding a parking space in San Francisco by 50%.

"I thought I would take you up the ridge road to 280 and then into the City. It should give you some fun views. Then when we come back on Sunday, I will take us down the coast if we have time."

I had already figured out that no matter where in the Bay Area people lived they referred to San Francisco as 'the City'.

"Sounds great, since I have no idea where we are going."

The tour proved to be a total joy. We started talking in the car about high school and college. I found it even easier to talk to Diana casually in the car than when we were working or sitting around in 'the kitchen'. She had a great way of listening and then asking for more details about what you were saying. I rather wished I was more like that.

There was a section of the ridge road high enough up that with one turn you were looking at the San Francisco Bay and on the next turn you were looking out over the Pacific Ocean. The bay side was filled with civilization (roads, houses, buildings), while the other side was nearly empty (just rolling hills all the way down to the coastline). It was quite a contrast.

We also had a nice view of San Francisco's airport with its 'famous' parallel runways which sometimes frightened people when they saw another plane landing at the same time as they were only a couple hundred feet away.

Once we got to San Francisco, Diana had everything perfectly planned. We started at the Civic Center with its ornate City Hall and the opera house and music halls. We drove along the wharf past the ferry building and the cruise ship docks and Fisherman's Wharf. I realized I was still the 'little kid' from Wisconsin and even though I had lived in Chicago and spent time in New York, the combination of palm trees and San Francisco sophistication was hard to describe and take in fully.

We also drove by the Janis Joplin and the Grateful Dead houses in the Haight Ashbury post hippie neighborhood. We went down crooked Lombard Street and up to Coit Tower. We stopped at Crissy Field on the way to the old civil war era Fort Point which sits directly under the Golden Gate Bridge. We walked around the back alleys of Chinatown, where it really does feel more like China than

California; 80% to 90% of the people on the street are Chinese.

We stood in Aquatic Park looking at Alcatraz Island, while Diana gave me her personal version of *Escape from Alcatraz*. I knew that the government's stance was still that no one ever escaped Alcatraz alive. But I also knew they admit that three prisoners did get off the island on a raft made out of wood and inflated cloth. They were never heard of again, and parts of the raft were recovered. Between the freezing cold water, the rip tides that sweep out into the Pacific Ocean and all of the sharks in the bay, the government stated publicly it was sure the escapees did not make it.

Then, Diana told me about the Dolphin Club which has a clubhouse right next to the park. They hold an annual *Escape From Alcatraz* triathlon. The contestants (men and women) are ferried to Alcatraz. They swim (no wetsuits) 1.5 miles to Aquatic Park. Then, they get on their bikes and ride across the Golden Gate Bridge to Mill Valley, a distance of 12 miles. At that point, they run up and down hills almost to Stinson Beach and back to Mill Valley, which is 14 miles. They have been holding this event since 1981, and nearly everyone finishes the swim portion, and no one has ever drowned or been attacked by sharks.

As Diana said, "But your government says it is sure that these three prisoners drowned. You can draw your own conclusion, but I think they made it."

I was totally charmed by both San Francisco and my tour guide.

In the early afternoon, we drove across the Golden Gate Bridge and parked on the other side. Then we walked halfway back. The view and the feeling on this bridge were amazing. For years, I had seen it in movies and on television, and now I was here… with Diana. I was starting to understand why San Francisco was considered the romantic city.

We continued on to Sausalito, now an expensive hillside community with the most spectacular view ever of San Francisco from across the bay. We ate a late lunch at one of the waterside restaurants built on piers over the water. I played tourist and ordered us crab and lobster and a couple glasses of wine. The sun was out, the food was great, the view was wonderful, I felt my head spinning a bit.

Maybe it was the wine... but I was thinking. *This might be the best lunch I have ever had…*

The smile on my face was also probably twice as big as usual.

Afterwards, we drove back to San Francisco to Diana's apartment. Her neighborhood is called the Marina and stands on the flat stretch of land that the Pan Pacific Exposition was built on in 1915 as a world's fair to show that San Francisco had come back from the deadly 1906 earthquake and fire.

She was right. With the Mini's size, we found a parking spot not far away. Her room was in an apartment that was on the third floor with most buildings being no more than four stories in this section of San Francisco.

The inside of the apartment was a nice size. Her roommate was not home. Diana showed me her room, which was very simply decorated. Again, almost no photos except for one of an older couple whom I guessed were her parents. I asked her how she had found such a nice place.

"Craigslist. I saw an ad for a room for rent. I knew I wanted to be in the Marina, so that made it easy. I did it a little over a year ago."

It was already 6:30 when we got to the apartment, and about 30 minutes later her roommate showed up.

"Jay, this is my roommate Kelly. Kelly, this is Jay."

Kelly was an example of what I discovered later was a frequent sight in the Marina, a cute, athletic, under thirty, single female. She came forward with her hand outstretched.

"Nice to meet you Jay. Diana told me you're taking advantage of our luxurious couch tonight."

Then she turned to Diana. "Are we still meeting everyone at Delarosa's at eight?"

"Yes. As far as I know. Why don't you take your shower first?"

"Sounds good," and off she went to her room.

Diana then asked, "Would you like some wine?"

I said yes and she got a couple glasses from the kitchen and put a bottle of pinot noir on the dining table. We talked about how much fun the 'tour' had been with Diana commenting that she had had a great time seeing things she hadn't seen in a while.

I was thinking… *This is one very special girl…*

The timing was tight with only one shower. But everything worked out, and I got a quick shower just before eight. Typical guy, I was ready five minutes later.

Delarosa's turned out to be an upscale pizza restaurant/bar on Chestnut Street, the main commercial street of the Marina. The street name reminded me of my 'new ride' at the Farm, Chestnut the horse.

We got there about fifteen minutes after eight and there was a line out the door already. Kelly spoke up, "I hope someone got here early enough to get us a table. I'll squeeze in and look."

We watched from the window and Diana leaned in toward me and said, "Kelly is pretty aggressive, and she usually gets what she is after." I looked up and saw her standing near a table with a couple empty seats talking to a couple of people at the table and then waving us in.

The seating a Delarosa's was mainly stools some big enough for two people to squeeze onto.

Over the next hour I met a number of Diana's friends. There were about twelve people - eight girls and four boys. I was seated next to Diana and across from Kelly. The pizza and wine kept coming, and at one point a second table was commandeered. I was having a great time, talking to Diana, meeting new people and asking questions of Kelly who had become a lot more 'chatty' the last hour. Perhaps it was the amount of wine she had consumed.

I was feeling great too … and then the roof fell in.

Three nice looking guys showed up at the table. Diana stood up and introduced me to them. I've forgotten two of their names, but the third was named Brian. Diana seemed a bit nervous when she introduced me to Brian. I was bit surprised as well that his greeting to Diana was a kiss on her lips and an arm placed around her.

Brian squeezed in on the other side of Diana and engaged her in some serious conversation. About ten minutes later, they both stood up, and Diana leaned over and said to Kelly and me.

"I'm heading out with Brian. I will catch up with you later." And then she was gone.

I am not sure now what I did at that point, but I think I probably just stared as they walked out of the restaurant together.

What was that? ...Who is this guy? ...

I looked over at Kelly and pointed toward Brian's back as he left. "Who is that?"

"Brian?" Kelly looked a bit confused. "That's Diana's boyfriend. Sometimes he shows up and sometimes he doesn't. Not a very nice guy if you ask me."

Just then one of girls from farther down the table slid over next to me, creating more space for the two guys who had showed up with Brian.

Boyfriend... what boyfriend? ....

I was starting to feel betrayed the way I felt about Rachel.

Just then someone put a couple bottles of wine and two pizzas down on our table, and Kelly picked up one of the bottles and held it out to me.

"Want a refill?"

I was still feeling sideswiped. "Ah… sure. Ah... yes definitely."

Kelly filled my glass and then hers. She went back to our earlier conversation and asked me what working in Chicago was like.

It helped right then to have someone to talk to no matter what the topic, so I focused on Kelly and her questions. The girl next to me seemed focused on the guy on the other side of her, so she didn't notice I was ignoring her (after all, she was ignoring me).

But I still couldn't get Brian's existence out of my mind. *Diana has a boyfriend? ... What were all the looks for?... Did I get this all wrong?...*

Kelly poured me another glass of wine. I seemed to be drinking it rather quickly, and that felt good. I asked her where she grew up (Orange County) and where she worked (Twitter).

A couple glasses of wine later, Kelly suggested we head back to the apartment. I agreed and somehow got to my feet. Kelly directed me out of the restaurant and on to the sidewalk. She propped me up, as we walked the four blocks to the apartment. She was busy telling me what she liked about living in San Francisco and what she didn't.

At some point, we reached the apartment and started climbing the stairs to the third floor. In my condition, those stairs seemed to go on forever. She was ahead of me, and I remember looking up from behind her thinking.

It must be all these stairs that give her those great legs ...

She unlocked the door, and I followed her in. I had no sooner closed the door than she turned and started to kiss me. And not gently, but rather passionately, with her arms tightly around my neck. I found myself kissing her back. It started as a reflex and then grew into something I was enjoying. Next, she started to unbutton my shirt. I should have done something, but I just let her take my shirt off while she kept kissing me. I was still standing by the door.

When my shirt was off, she grabbed my hand and led me down the hall into her bedroom and down on the bed. While I can remember the 'highlights', I certainly do not remember all of the next hour. But needless to say, when I woke up in the morning, I was lying next to Kelly and neither one of us had on any clothes.

I was thinking fuzzy when I first woke up, and I certainly had no idea what time it was. I was also confused about what I should do next. Don't get me wrong. I had had one-night stands in college, but it had been a while. And I had never had one with my 'friendly' co-worker's roommate and then need to ride home with her that same afternoon. Not to mention need to work with her over the next couple of months.

This is a pretty dumb position to be in... and then it occurred to me... *Diana's not here... and probably will not be for a while...* That thought hurt.

I found a clock. It said 10:30, and I wasn't sure just how late Diana would be, so I started to get out of bed. Just then Kelly opened her eyes.

She smiled at me and said, "That was great last night."

Now what do you say to respond to that?...

"Yes it was. Unexpected, but fun." *Not bad for a quick response from a fuzzy brain.*

"If you're getting up, can you go the bakery on Chestnut and get us coffee and something to eat?"

I stood up and put my clothes on. "Sure. Is the shop straight up Scott Street?"

"Yes and just get the coffee black. I have the cream and sugar here."

With that, I was out of the bedroom and then out of the apartment and heading to the bakery.

What was I thinking last night?... Obviously, I wasn't thinking...

I decided to try one of Russ's keys. It seemed the right time and place to Forgive, Forget, Move on. I certainly could forgive myself for a weak moment. Yet I was still feeling blindsided by Diana.

How did I misread her so badly?...

As for Forget, with Kelly, there wasn't really anything to forget. But with Diana there was. I had to forget that I was feeling alive with her. I had to move on. She was just being a friend. It had been my mistake. By the time I reached the bakery, I was starting to get my head around all that had happened in the past day.

The line at the bakery was long, and even in my preoccupied, fuzzy state, I noticed that the line was all 20 to 35 year olds, and two-thirds were girls.

They're everywhere around here...

My mind was really mixed up after the last 24 hours…

I bought the coffee and a bunch of different pastry. I had no idea what Kelly might like.

Walking back, I thought maybe Diana would not find out about last night. But part of me wanted her to find out. I was still feeling hurt by my misreading of our relationship.

Then I remembered Alicia's comments. She had noticed the same thing. It wasn't just me. That made me mad all over again. And that is the way I entered the apartment.

When I opened the door, I could hear the water in the shower running, so I went to the kitchen to put the coffee and food down. And there was Diana sitting having a glass of orange juice. I was totally startled.

"Ah… I didn't know you were here…. I… just went out for coffee and pastries." I put my two bags on the table and opened them. "Would you like any?"

Diana looked at me and said. "No thanks. I'm not hungry this morning."

I didn't know what to do or say at this point. I was mad at her, and yet I liked her, and I was totally embarrassed about sleeping with her roommate – all at the same time.

Finally I tried to offer an explanation, "Listen, I want… ah… apologize for…" But before I could finish, Diana cut me off.

"No need to apologize."

That sure cuts that problem off….she could care less what I do…

Diana continued, "She's like that. I probably should have mentioned it, but… I didn't think it would happen so

179

quickly… and frankly, I didn't think I would be gone so long."

So much for the boyhood charm… Kelly had picked me up. That was clear, and apparently she wasn't too picky…

Then Diana continued a bit too matter-of-factly, "Listen. I'm meeting a couple of artist friends of Russ's daughter, Monique, for lunch in an hour. Do you want to join me or…. ah... stay here with Kelly? I'm fine either way. Your choice."

I didn't really want to go with Diana, but at this point I really didn't want to stay with Kelly either.

"Sounds good, I'll join you," I answered. "I still need a shower. Do I have time for that?"

"We don't need to leave for another half hour or so. They live in Dog Patch, and we can drive the Mini there and then head back to the Farm afterwards. Okay?"

Dog Patch… what kind of place is called Dog Patch?…

"Sounds good," Apparently, my vocabulary was restricted to two words as a result of my mixed emotions.

Other than a couple of slightly embarrassing moments with Kelly, my escape from the apartment was uneventful and I joined Diana in her car. As we rode to Dog Patch, she described more of the San Francisco neighborhoods.

I was not paying much attention, however, as I was still trying to process all the changes to what I thought reality had been. As Russ would say, I was trying to 'adjust to the new reality'. Mainly, I had to realize that Diana had a boyfriend.

Then another 180 degree shift happened.

Diana said, "I just wanted to apologize again for leaving you at dinner last night."

Why is she apologizing... again...? It just raised my anger again, that I hadn't known about her boyfriend.

"Well your boyfriend showed up. What were you to do?" I might have sounded a bit sarcastic, but I tried not to be attacking.

"Ex-boyfriend..."

Ex-boyfriend??? My mind was stunned.

"I broke up with him last night.... It has been coming on for a few weeks, but I had decided to finalize it last night... It took longer than I thought it would."

What?... no boyfriend... anymore...

Now I really felt stupid about spending the night with Kelly... her roommate.

Shit, I really screwed this up...

"I think I see a parking spot." She immediately changed the topic. If you have ever tried to find a parking space in San Francisco, you know how 'top of the list' that topic can be.

Lunch was a bit of a blur for me. Once again, my reality had shifted. I wondered how much trouble my night with Kelly had caused.

As we drove home, Diana used the Coast Road and gave me another geography and history lesson. We even stopped in Moss Beach to explore the tide pools. A Wisconsin boy generally does not know much about tide pools, so it was all interesting.

When we got back to the Farm, Diana was still nice to me, but I could sense a bit more formal. She opened the front door, turned off the alarm system, and turned on the lights. She then asked if I wanted an early dinner. She was sure there were plenty of leftovers to choose from.

I said 'sure' and we went down to the kitchen and found plenty of variety. We sat at the counter, and I asked her about Lynn and Russ. It seemed like a safe topic.

It was. Diana couldn't think more highly of either one of them. At one point, when she was describing how supportive they were of each other, she looked away for a second and then said it was that supportiveness or lack of it from Brian that was one of the big deciding reasons she had decided to break up with him. When she saw Lynn and Russ together, she can see how easily they could grow old together.

They are not going to grow old together…

I was immediately stabbed with guilt. I knew about Russ dying, and Diana didn't. I was also struck by how devastating that loss was going to be for Lynn…

"Chocolate cake?" Diana got up and took her plate to the dishwasher.

"Sounds great." Boy, was I in a 'rut'. I was giving that same response to everything Diana said…

She brought over a huge piece of cake and three scoops of ice cream. Her serving was less than half mine.

I pointed it out. "But, you're a growing boy." And she laughed.

While we enjoyed the cake, somehow I managed to ask. "What is your favorite game in the game room?"

She answered immediately, "Ms Pac-Man."

"Ooh… that sounds a bit like a challenge."

"You could take it that way… if you want." She looked me straight in the eye.

"You're on."

With that exchange, we headed over to the game room. I was really starting to like this room.

After she beat me three straight times, I smiled and asked, "Okay... You win. What is your second favorite game here?"

"I'm not any good at it, but I have always liked darts."

"Darts?"

"Yes, darts. Why, have you never played?" She countered.

"Yes, but only in bars."

"Me too," she added with a wink and headed over to the dartboard area.

Needless to say she had sandbagged me. She was twice as good as I was.

Then she said, "This was fun, but I have an early morning call with the Paris office, so I think I should be off to bed. I didn't sleep well last night."

I quickly thought to myself... *Do not say 'sounds good' one more time, you idiot...*

And I didn't. "I think I'm going to practice Ms Pac-Man for a while. I'll see you in the morning."

I do not need an awkward moment in front of her cottage... too much has happened in too short an amount of time...

"You need more than practice." She responded with a laugh and headed out the door.

I had a great time playing several of the old popular arcade games. After about an hour I went down to my cottage. I noticed the lights were off in #1.

14

The kids came back on Monday afternoon and until my Wednesday ride with Alicia, nothing much happened, except for the surprise I had for Kevin at dinner on Monday. On Monday morning I had received an email from my internet radio buddy, Jeremy, asking if This Kid had any more songs.

I had forgotten that I had sent the one song to him last week – a lot had been happening in my own life…

Since Jeremy was asking for more songs, I assumed he must have liked the first song, but I still wrote back to ask him 'how much' he liked it.

He replied. "In one week, This Kid is #28 and climbing on our Electronic Music station. Does he have more?"

I knew he was talking about Kevin's song, but it took me a minute to figure out who This Kid was.

Jeremy??? Who is This Kid?…

I would have been clueless, but the email thread still had my original email. In it, I had not referred to Kevin by his name. I had just said a song from 'This kid I know' and by mistake capitalized the T. Jeremey must have thought that 'This Kid' was the artist's stage name.

I had no idea how good being #28 on his station was, so I asked. Jeremy responded and said it was the fastest rising song from an unknown artist in at least three years. In other words, Kevin had a hit…

I did not commit a second song to Jeremy. While I felt Kevin would be pleased about his song's popularity, I hadn't asked for permission to send it to Jeremy. And... Jeremy had played it publicly without my permission.

I went to the radio website, found the top 40 list, and printed it with #28 reading This Kid. The song name was equally weird. Kevin apparently didn't think of names, so he had just numbered his songs on his saved file on his Mac. This song just happened to be #13.

After everyone was seated for dinner, I asked Kevin if he remembered sending his songs to me. I knew he did, but I wanted to start the conversation somewhere.

"Yeah," he answered.

"I have this friend, Jeremy, who works for an Internet radio station. I sent your song to him last week to get his opinion."

Kevin brightened immediately. "What did he say?"

"I'm pretty sure he thought it was excellent."

"You're 'pretty sure'… what did he actually say?" Kevin was getting a bit suspicious.

"It's not what he said, Kevin, but rather what he did." I continued, "He thought enough of it that without my permission he played it on their Electronic Music channel."

I took the printed page out and put it in front of Kevin. "And this is what happened… By the way, he did not understand my email and thought your stage name was This Kid and that the name of the song was #13."

Before he looked at the paper, Kevin looked up at me and said. "I haven't named any of my songs. I just number them." Then he looked down at the paper and read it slowly. I guess he wanted to make sure what he was reading.

"This list says my song is #28 on their list of requested music. Is that good?"

"Yes Kevin. That is very good." I pointed to the #30 song. "You're currently two songs ahead of Moby…"

"Cool." Kevin said, and then he added. "I kind of like the 'This Kid' name. Can I use it?"

"I would think so. I don't think anyone famous is using it."

"You're my lawyer, so you should know... right?"

Got to love nine year olds… Too much television is all I can think of …

Alex spoke up, "Can I see that list?" Kevin handed him the list.

Alex looked at it for a second then said, "This is awesome." Then he looked me and asked, "Can I tell my friends about this at school?"

Good question…

"Ah… maybe we should wait a couple of days on that. I didn't know my friend Jeremy was going to do what he did, and I think we had better 'clear' this with GP first. I don't see why not, but I could be wrong."

Diana leaned over to Alex and asked if she could see the list too. Holding the list in her hand, she looked at Kevin and said, "Amazing, Kevin. Can I listen to the song?"

"Sure." He reached into his pocket and pulled out his iPod. He played with it a bit. Apparently it was connected to one of the speakers on a shelf near the dining table because the song began to play from there. Kevin increased the volume which it made it easy to hear, but hard to talk.

When the song was over, Alex said, "Kevin, that is really good. How did you do it?"

"I just used the music program on my Mac plus the digital Mixcraft software I got for Christmas last year."

The conversation continued for the whole rest of dinner and moved into the game room where Alex trounced me once again in air hockey.

Wednesday afternoon was my ride with Alicia. Again she showed herself as a twelve-year old who was operating as if she were already twenty-two.

After she did a couple of circuits of jumps, she and Bronco came out of the jumping arena and over to where Chestnut and I were waiting. "Do you want to do one of the three rides we have already done again or try something new?"

I thought for a minute and couldn't decide. Alicia was watching me struggle. So she said.

"Do you want me to decide?"

"Ah... sure"

"Let's go to the beach again."

As we rode down to the beach, she did her usual Alicia thing, and asked me all kinds of questions. "Were you having trouble making a decision on where to ride today?"

"Ah... yes. I guess so," I responded.

"I can see that GP hasn't taught you the three decision system yet."

What three decision system??

"Ah… no" *What twelve year old can get me to every answer with 'Ah'…*

"It really helps you to make decisions…"

"Basically, GP says that there are only three types of decisions. Type one is for big, important decisions. There aren't too many of these, so you can spend a lot of time figuring out what to do."

"Type two is for small decisions that will repeat many times, like what is the fastest way to drive from here to school for example – these you can spend some time figuring out the best answer for."

"And the last type is for all the rest or any decision that is not a type one or two. And for these decisions, you should spend almost no time figuring them out. Like where to ride today. GP says that even if which way we go could eventually be important, because it seemed like a minor decision when we were deciding it's still best to do it quickly."

"Once you get used to doing it, the three decision system makes things real easy. You stop worrying about which movie to go to and just pick one and go. It's no big deal…"

Another Russ lesson on how to make living easier so you can enjoy life. I'll have to remember to write this one down.

 But I just said, "Got it."

The beach ride was as much fun as the first time. I was feeling more comfortable on Chestnut and we could chase after Alicia and Bronco a bit more.

When we returned to the stable, I watched the rapport Alicia and Bronco had. She would happily talk his ears off, and he would look at her and occasionally shake his head and wiggle his ears.

Her one true friend… it's good to have one… I will get another one someday….

Lynn and Russ returned after dinner on Thursday, and they were full of stories about all the fun that they had in Maui. Lynn's favorite was Russ's surfing excursion.

"So we climb down this steep hill to the best surf spot on the west side of Maui. I keep thinking Russ is going to kill himself carrying this huge surfboard that he rented." Lynn uses her hands and arms to convey the size of the board.

"We finally get down to the beach and there are lots of people there, probably ten to fifteen in the water and more on the beach. There were too many twenty-year-old hard bodies in bikinis. I had to work hard to get Russ to stop staring and get in the water."

Russ just shrugged his shoulders and smiled at this comment.

"There were two break points and Russ said he would just do the easier one. So he paddled out. I saw he was at least three times the age of anyone out there. I'm not sure what they thought when they saw him."

"Anyway he caught a couple of waves and I could see that paddling back out was getting harder for him. But he decided to paddle over to the bigger break, the much bigger break. I started thinking 'should I dial 911 now or wait for the accident to actually happen.' "

"One of the beach babes made a comment about the 'old guy' trying the big waves and half the beach crowd was now watching him."

"There were only three guys doing the bigger waves, so when Russ got there they talked to him. I assumed they were telling him to go back and do the smaller waves. But, oh no, they were telling him how to catch the break."

Russ gave Lynn's arm a hug and smiled 'innocently' again.

"Well, the next set came in and two of the guys tried to catch the first wave. Russ and the other guy waited for the second one."

"The two guys on the first wave missed it and therefore were just sitting in the water when the second wave came along." Both Russ and the other guy caught the second wave. Very quickly they were bearing down on the first two."

"Russ cut his board in between the two, and the other guy went over the top to be safe. Russ handled the wave and ended with a classic drop and paddled in."

"I notice two things… First, he was so tired he could hardly carry his board. Second, he was trying hard to suck in his stomach and puff out his chest, as he walked past the bikini crowd. All I could think about was 'once a male, always a male."

"We stayed for a while just to watch before heading up the hill. The three guys from the big break came up to us and congratulated Russ on his ride. They said he was one of the oldest guys to ever try it."

"Russ's ego might have been difficult to handle after that, except for the fact that he was so tired that he needed me to help him carry the board back up the hill."

Russ finally commented, "Hey, I just decided I needed to do one wave with the 'big boys', and I lucked out. I didn't need a second wave. Hey… you have to know 'when to hold 'em and when to fold 'em'."

They talked more about the beach scene at the surf spot, and then Russ turned to me.

"How about going surfing tomorrow morning?"

Me?… surfing?… you got to be kidding…

"Ah… I've never surfed before, so I think I should pass."

"Jay, this is exactly when I think you need to say 'yes'… I have found that when I say 'yes' to things just outside my comfort zone, I experience more new things, increase my knowledge, and often add to my ability to be happy. Everybody is different. They have their own comfort zone."

"So Jay, how far out in your comfort zone is surfing?"

When put like that, it seemed silly to say no. So I said yes. Russ said the waves would be good at about 9 a.m. so we would leave the house at 8:30.

After a few more stories, I excused myself to head down to the cottage. I added the 'yes theory' to my journal and then got my Dick Francis book out to read some more.

The story was good enough to keep me wanting to read it…
Guess that is the definition of a good book.

15

Surfing turned out to be a blast with Russ. Why should I have been surprised… with his attitude, shoveling snow might become fun.

We loaded his pickup truck with wet suits and long boards. He told me long boards are pretty easy to stand up on and are the best learning boards for adults. On the drive down he described a bit of the technique, but said it would be much easier to show me once we were in the water. When we got to a place where a few cars were already parked, I saw a small dirt road heading down another 300 to 400 yards toward the beach.

Russ said, "See that gate there?"

"Yes"

"It has a padlock on it." He handed me a key. "This key will unlock it. After I pull through, please close and lock the gate."

I did that and got back in the car, and Russ explained. "This is an example of rules getting in the way of life. I bought this land many years ago for the express purpose of making sure this beach was available for surfers. But if I open it up and let everyone park on it so they are close to the beach, my insurance rate will go up by tens of thousands of dollars a year. As it is, because I am aware that people do trespass, every couple of years I have to hire a guard to stop anyone from trespassing. Otherwise I would permanently lose the easement over the land."

"Prescriptive easement," I said. "We studied about it in real estate law class. This is the first live case I have actually seen."

We parked the truck, put on our wet suits and went down to the beach. Russ told me to bring my board, and we walked into the water to a spot where the waves were small, and no one was surfing. He got me up on the first wave and I rode it pretty much up on the beach.

We kept trying bigger waves and moved slowly closer to where the real surfers were riding waves, but we never got there. Surfing is hard work, and I eventually wore out. I was sitting on the sand when Russ came up and said, "That was a great first day, especially for an adult."

"Thanks. Surfing's great fun," I said.

"Are you happy you said 'yes'?"

"Yes," I replied with a big smile.

Russ sat down next to me on the sand, and we just stared out at the waves crashing on the shore.

Then he said, "I love to just sit here and listen to the waves as they hit the beach. I like to watch the water foam up. It reminds me how insignificant I am in the grand scheme of life."

"I think it's important that people are honest about their faults. One of my biggest faults is my ego. Too often, I think I am right, and so I talk too much. And when I am talking I am not listening enough. I have made lots of mistakes because of that trait. You can see it when I play the Word game with the kids. As bad as it is now, I was worse when I was younger. I could be really obnoxious."

"So watching the power of an endless series of waves reminds me that I am as important as a grain of sand on the beach…" Then he added, "That and having Lynn kick me under the table when I have talked too much. That's a great reminder too." He smiled.

Listening to Russ talk about his faults was enough to humble me…

It turned out that Russ was going to San Francisco to pick up the twins, who were going to spend a week with us. It was spring break, and Monique had decided to go to an art show in New York. Mark's three kids were coming as well. Russ wasn't sure who was bringing a friend and for how long, but he figured that we probably would have ten to twelve kids in the house for most of the week.

He is so excited… I can tell he planned all this to happen at once…

I again felt sad that this might be the last time Russ would have all his grandchildren in the house at the same time. But his excitement was genuine, and it was his amazing ability to not let something in the past or future ruin today.

It really works for him….

When we got back to the house, we hosed down our suits and boards. I went to my cottage to change. I had a couple of hours of work I needed to get done. Then I noticed I was whistling in the shower. Having some fun each day sure made me happier.

After I got dressed, I checked my email and saw one from Jeremy. He was reporting that This Kid song #13 had climbed up the chart to #20. Again, he wanted to know if there were more songs. I had forgotten to bring that up to Russ, so I made a mental note to do it later today, maybe when he came back with the twins.

Dinner that night was indeed interesting. Anna again had gone with burger night, this time with a huge Chef's salad to go with it. The twins, Charlotte and Estelle, each brought a friend, different from the previous weekend. I also met Russ's son Mark's three kids.

Dan, the eighteen-year old, had already been accepted at Vanderbilt University with a partial tennis scholarship. He was an excellent doubles player. It became apparent very quickly that Dan had a special attachment to Kevin. Dan's buddy, Brent, came in his own car, and they were going to stay in cottage #7 next to me.

Loren was fifteen, but unlike the twins, she was still happy to be a teenager. She apparently was the star of the Los Gatos freshman girls' soccer team, and her athletic appearance fit her. She had brought a friend of hers from the soccer team. I expected to see them in the game room much of the time

At twelve, Marci was the same age as Alicia, but there was a great deal of difference between them. Marci's favorite pastime was music and musicians. She knew all the latest songs and up-and-coming artists as well as an amazing amount of rock and roll history back to the 1950's.

Alex had also brought a friend, Josh, for part of the week. That made thirteen kids in the house. It wasn't going to be quiet very often. I knew that.

The table had been expanded to accommodate eighteen people. Russ had helped Anna set up two lines for food, so everyone was able to sit down before any of the burgers got cold. When Anna finally sat, almost a universal feeding frenzy began. The kids were starving. Nearly everyone had their mouths full, it was temporarily pretty quiet. Russ chose this moment to speak up.

"I doubt it's really my turn for the Word, but as the oldest person at the table…"

"By far." It was Lynn seated next to Russ, interrupting to give him a bit of a hard time.

Russ put his hand gently on Lynn's shoulder "Ah… yes dear, by far… And…" looking directly at Lynn with a smile he continued. "As I was saying, I want to try out a Word before giving Kevin his chance as the youngest here."

They are such a great couple… how do I find someone like that??? Maybe I have…

"My Word tonight is 'believe in yourself' which I think is a highly important to being happy. I think it's especially helpful when you're a teenager."

"Who can give me a quick definition?"

Alicia raised her hand quickly.

"Okay Alicia." Russ responded.

"I think it means thinking you can do something even when not all the evidence points in that direction."

I thought for a second about how she said that… she definitely could speak her thoughts with precision.

Russ also pondered her answer for a second, and then said, "Ah… I think you answered that better than I was going to."

He continued, "Believing in yourself is probably not something anyone can teach you. It's more your attitude toward yourself. But one of the best ways of believing in yourself is not letting failure bother you."

"I mean, basically there are two things that can happen when you believe in yourself. Either you succeed or you fail. So if you can get over failure, then believing in yourself the next time becomes much easier. I think most of you know me as a very optimistic person. It is true I am. But, that is not through success, it's through not letting failure bother me."

"For example, I have tried to start dozens of companies during my life, and three out of four of them have failed. And despite that track record, I keep starting things, and every time I start something, I am still very confident that it will be a success, even if I know the 'odds' are against me."

"My favorite failure story is Thomas Edison and the light bulb. Apparently, he was interviewed after failing in his attempt to perfect the light bulb more than one thousand times. He was asked if he felt like a failure. His answer was 'No'. He had just discovered over a thousand ways not to make a light bulb'. Now that was a guy who truly believed in himself."

"My advice then is simple. Practice having confidence in yourself. Be your biggest cheerleader when you do something right. Your reward will be a happier you."

"Any thoughts anyone?"

Alex spoke up, "But what if you really know that you have no chance? Like a Spanish test or something. What do you do then?

"What is the best grade you think you can get?"

"If I am totally lucky, a B."

"Then start believing you can get a B and study to get a B. Got it?"

"Got it."

After dinner, I had berries and ice cream again with Russ, Lynn and Diana. The kids had left for the game room en masse. Somehow it felt like I was with Diana. And I listened as she told a story to Lynn about my bewitchment by Alicia.

At least she doesn't totally hate me for my drunken night with Kelly… wonder why… either she doesn't care –

which would not be good... or she uses Russ's forgive, forget, move on method...

When the berries and ice cream were gone, Russ announced he was going in to give Alex a thrashing in air hockey. With a smile, I accused him of believing too much in his abilities. Maybe he should scale back to believing he could win a game or two.

I went with Russ and when I entered the game room, it reminded me of the chaos of Chuck E Cheese. There was lots of yelling and game noise.

Before I knew it, Russ was in the middle of the kids with his first challenge ping pong with Dan. I noticed Dan was very good at ping pong. I found out later that most tennis players are also good at ping pong, apparently due to a similar hand-eye coordination skill – which I did not have. I skipped ping pong.

It was fun to watch Russ interact with all the kids. I think Diana was right. He was the biggest kid in the family. At one point, he was bowling with Dan and his friend, then in an air hockey challenge tournament with Alex and me, and afterwards playing darts with Marci, Alicia and Diana. Then he was running to the kitchen to get more snacks for everyone. I don't think I'd ever seen him happier.

16

On Saturday, I ended up riding with both Marci and Alicia. Because of frequent visits to the Farm, Marci was good with a horse, even if not as good as Alicia. We rode up to Margie's Peak and had another lunch. Alicia was 'demonstrating' her knowledge of me to Marci by asking questions she already knew the answer to like 'Did I miss the snow in Wisconsin?', 'No'.

Marci just seemed happy to let Alicia take the lead, and she asked me more about what movies I liked. She engaged in as much music and movie talk as she could. With the Academy Awards just a few weeks earlier, she wanted to know my favorites. Then she moved on to music, asking all kinds of questions about the music I liked. I asked if she had heard Kevin's new song.

"What song? Kevin… Kevin made a song?" Marci had not heard about it yet.

Alicia took over and told her all about Kevin's song and my sending it to a radio station. Marci wanted to hear it as soon as we got back to the house.

Coming down from Margie's Peak was the same slow process for the horses. They picked out the best places to put their hoofs. While we were single file, Alicia engaged Bronco in a one-sided conversation. Marci leaned over to me once and told me, "She really loves that horse." I nodded in agreement.

After caring for the horses, Marci drove us back to the house. Alicia told her to drop me at my cottage. I went in and relaxed for a while, then called my mother and checked in. She told me she was doing 'fine', but I sensed a bit of weariness in her voice. So I pushed a bit more.

She explained. "I miss you some. I know it has only been a few weeks, but I sort of got used to you living in the house again."

It's hard to hear you are making someone that you love feel sad even if you are doing so simply by not being there.

Visit…She can come for a visit…

"Mom. I just had a thought… Come visit us here at the house. Maybe come at the end of my visit when I don't have any work left for Uncle Russ, and we can just explore the area."

She was at first hesitant, but then I assured her that Russ would be happy to see her and loved visitors. At the end of our call, she at least agreed to think about it.

I went up to the house an hour before dinner that night and joined Alex, Josh, Dan, Brent, Russ and Kevin in a long game of horse. Kevin was given double letters and half the distance. Still at age nine, it was tough for Kevin.

The more I watched Russ, the more I realized he was just having fun. He wasn't playing with the kids to impress them or get 'quality time' with them or to try any 'new age' parenting approach. He was playing because he liked doing it. I noticed the kids could tell. And that made them want to play with him even more. He had created a virtuous cycle where everyone ends up a bit happier than before.

Dinner that night was 'make your own' salad night. It was better than any restaurant 'salad bar' I had ever been to. I also noticed for the first time that while there were no rules, almost everyone showed up for dinner together, even the 'twins'. It meant that they were attracted to what happened at dinner and didn't feel compelled to attend.

I asked Russ about that later in the week, and once again he gave me a valuable insight (which I wrote in my journal that night.) He said that Sting had an old song that said it best, 'If you love someone, set them free.'

The basic concept is that if you give someone the freedom to do something, including the freedom to love you or not love you, then two things occur. First, you (or in this case, a family dinner) become more attractive simply by your letting go instead of trying to control someone. Secondly, if they still want to be with you, then you know that choice is truly genuine.

Everyone's salad was different. Some people made cool wedge salads, some a simple chicken Caesar, and some a combination of everything they liked (that was me). It looked like a mess, but I loved it.

After everyone started eating, Russ 'announced' that he and Kevin had devised a short music quiz instead of the Word game.

"Kevin is going to play part of a song and see if you can guess who the musician is. Sort of a Farm version of 'Name that Tune.' "

Russ and Kevin then played four songs. The last was Human After All by Daft Punk and almost all the kids knew that one.

Then Russ said, "Okay. Next we're going to play two new songs and when they are both done, I want you to vote which one you like better. If you know who the artist is, please don't say."

I think I know these two songs… I had a small smile on my face.

I was right. These were the two best songs that Kevin had created. Kevin played the one I had sent to the radio station first. After they were both over, Russ asked for a show of hands as to who liked which song the most. There was only a one vote difference. Of course, Marci voted for both songs…

People started commenting about which song was better and then Russ pulled out the paper showing Kevin's song at #20 and announced, "Both these songs were created by Kevin, and thanks to Jay, one of them has been on Internet radio and is now the twentieth most requested song on the station." He laid the paper down on the table.

There was on moment of silence, and then Dan started to clap. The others joined in, and then Dan stood up and kept clapping. Quickly everyone joined him in standing.

After the excitement died down a bit Dan asked, "Hey Kevin, was this your first standing ovation?"

Kevin thought a second and then said, "Ah… yeah."

"It is one more than I've ever gotten." Dan reached over the table and gave Kevin a high five.

I was impressed how Dan went out of his way to make Kevin feel good about himself. I wondered if there was something about Kevin that Dan saw and wanted to help out with. Or was this just Dan being Dan and helping the people around him feel good made him feel good?

I'm sure if I ask Russ he would tell me which it is... but whichever, it does seem to make both of them happy...

It was now Marci's turn for the Word. She simply asked, "Why is music important?"

The way she phrased the question, it was obvious that she thought music was important and just wanted to hear why others thought it was.

Lynn jumped right in, "Can I handle this one?"

Russ smiled, "Please be my guest."

Lynn launched her reply by saying that there were two things she thought about when Marci asked her question. One was that music is a form of art. And that art in the broadest sense is part of what all humans can appreciate rather than just live lives of only work and food and more work and more food.

But then she said that in her opinion music is also a way of storing a memory. As we grow older, we notice more and more that certain music reminds us of certain events or periods in our lives and the music brings these memories out whenever we hear those songs.

Everyone had fun with the topic. Dan chimed in that rock stars can be rich and asked Kevin what he would do with all the money he was going to make…

Post dinner, we enjoyed a combination of movies and games. The first movie was *Dead Poets Society,* which Russ said was a must see for any teenager. The second movie was *Ferris Bueller's Day Off*, another classic teenage movie. Some watched one movie, some watched both, and some watched neither. The 'no rules' set them free and worked as usual. Everybody figured out what they wanted the most, and thus there was no fighting, no complaints - no problems. I think the third movie was *Die Hard 3*, but I was in bed long before that one started.

The whole week went pretty much this same way. Many of the friends had to go back to their homes during the week, so by Friday it was just the grandchildren with the exception of Brent who seemed to be in heaven at the Farm. He also seemed especially pleased that Estelle had a crush on him. From my point of view she looked to have an interest, but 'crush' would be an overstatement. In any event, Brent was a typical male, and his ego grew with every glance she gave him.

The tension between Alicia and Charlotte was softened by the appearance of Marci. It gave someone for

Alicia to be with and lessened her need to worry about Charlotte. I rode a couple more times with both Alicia and Marci on the beach. The conversations were interesting. Mainly, Alicia was telling Marci that she wasn't sure she would ever be interested in boys. Even with me there, she declared, "Maybe I'm a lesbian. Jay, how would I know?"

What would I know??? She really means it... What do I say?...

"I don't really know. I mean, at some point I was attracted to girls. And... I guess I mean attracted in a different way than just being friends. I wanted to kiss them, at least, some of them. Actually, now that I think about it, I wanted to kiss only a few of them. But I can say that I never felt that way toward any boy. So I am guessing it's the same if you're gay or lesbian, only different of course."

"Got it – thanks." And with that, she changed the subject.

So did that really help her?... or did she just say 'got it' because it all was worthless and she wanted to move on?...

I noticed that no matter who was riding with us, Alicia always talked to Bronco and treated him special. He was her one true friend as she said. It seemed to work for her.

I was working with Russ in his office on Thursday afternoon when Dan came in.

"GP, can I ask you for some advice?" he said before he saw me in the corner looking for a file. "Oh, Jay, I didn't see you there. I didn't mean to interrupt or anything."

Russ answered quickly, "No problem, Dan. Come sit here." He pointed to the other chair at the window where he was sitting – with his usual open diet coke of course. "Don't worry about Jay. He's our lawyer, so anything you say is subject to attorney client privilege. That means he can't tell anyone unless you're planning to commit murder or something like that."

Dan sat down. "No, it's nothing like that. It's just my mom. I don't know how to handle her."

"Ah… what do you mean by 'handle'?"

"Well… she's trying to run everything in my life. The latest bit was her trying to pick my roommate at college. Vanderbilt has a program for that with the sports teams, and she wants to pick my roommate. I just need her to stop."

"Ah… This is one of the most difficult problems with life. You're hoping that an important person in your life will change their behavior… Let me put it bluntly, Dan They won't change.

Now it's true, people do change, but in my experience, trying to make someone change is almost impossible. Looking at my friends, occasionally they change because they want to change. But more often, they change without really being aware they are changing. So this can become a serious problem for your happiness."

Dan responded. "It is right now. I know it should get better when I'm at school, but that's six months from now, and for all I know she will be in Nashville every other weekend."

Russ laughed. "She just might...' Then he quickly added. "I'm kidding, Dan."

"Well, I'm not."

"Okay you asked for advice, so here goes... First, do not try to change other people in the ways you wish they would change. The easiest way to deal with this issue is to avoid getting involved with people who have serious things you think they need to change for you to be happy. This is extremely true when picking a wife for example. But it also works for avoiding problem friends, problem bosses, etc."

"Now, your mother, you cannot avoid her.... first accept reality. She will not change no matter how hard you try. Of course, she might change, but if that is your way of dealing with this issue, I think you're up for a major failure.

Russ continued, "So that leaves it up to what 'you' can do, not what 'she' can do. In your case, you can focus on the fact that in six months you will have 2,000 miles between

.t will make a major difference. I daresay it will

hange your relationship with your mother and nearly everyone else in your life. It does for most college kids who leave home."

Dan responded, "I know, but what about now? What can I do now?"

"As my Dad used to tell me, you can 'grin and bear it' and still be happy. It's like having a cast on a broken arm. Knowing how long you have to have that cast helps you put up with it and not let it get you down too much. Same thing applies to your mother. I'm sure you find 'battling' her only makes things worse. Like fights and stuff?"

"Yeah… it can really get bad."

"Remember this is all up to you, not her." Russ paused. "So try to take her 'meddling' and flip it in your brain. Try to see it all as her way of loving you instead of trying to control you… which it may actually be. Then, instead of fighting back, just thank her as if she just said 'I love you'. This way you are in control of your feelings, not your mother. I think you'll feel a lot better about yourself too once you feel in control of your emotions."

They talked some more about Dan's mother, Dan's going away to college and life in general. After Dan left, I asked Russ. "Where do you come up with all these ideas anyway?"

"I'm old," he said with a big smile.

That's right to the point.

He continued. "With any luck at all, you will be my age someday. And you'll be able to look back at all the things that have happened during your life and use them to make better decisions. I slowly discovered that most any misery I suffered was mainly self-inflicted. I learned that the AA Serenity Prayer is one of the keys to happiness for anyone. Do you know the Serenity Prayer?"

Is he in AA?... Is that why he never drinks?

I had heard 'of' it, but I was not sure I had actually ever heard it.

"No. I've heard it mentioned, but I do not really know anything about it."

"It's a simple, but powerful, concept." He paused as if he was trying to remember it. Then he said, " 'God, grant me the serenity to accept the things I cannot change, the courage to change the things I can, and the wisdom to know the difference'."

"I discovered that the list of things I could change was small and nearly all centered on how I viewed the world and the actions I took because of that view. So, I now simply approach every problem with that in mind. My 'accept reality' approach is really the same as the first line of the Serenity Prayer. I didn't realize it for years until one day a friend of mine who is in AA told the prayer to me."

Just then I saw Russ wince in pain.

"Are you Okay?" He held up his hand with one figure up.

So it hurts too much to talk... boy that was fast...

I had not seen Russ have a pancreatic attack before, but I guessed that was what was happening. A minute went by and Russ seemed to relax a bit

"Sorry about that. It was my pancreas acting up a bit."

"Ah... yes. Is there anything I can get you?"

"No, no... It was just a minor attack. It hurt a bit, but it was very short. So other than losing my breath for a bit, I should be fine in about thirty minutes. Just go ahead and finish those files, I will come back and answer questions when I feel better.

"Okay." I went back to my office. However, I couldn't focus on my work. My only thought was... *It really is happening...* I realized I needed to somehow get past this. Then it dawned on me. Russ had just given me the tools to do that.

Accept reality... He is dying and nothing can be done.

Change what I can change… which is my view of that reality. Russ doesn't want a bunch of sad people around. He wants to live his life to the fullest as long as possible. I need to be happy with every day I have with him. If it wasn't for his 'out of the blue' call, I never would have even known him. I am lucky to be here at all…

The more I thought about that call, the more I wondered about how it came about. How exactly did Russ know I was in need of a change? *I will have to ask him someday… someday soon…*

17

The rest of the week went by quickly. I worked, I surfed, I worked some more, I rode horses, I worked even more, and I played a lot of games with the kids. Then it was Saturday.

Saturday night was going to be quite the dinner. The twins' mother, Monique, had arrived Friday night and was staying until Sunday evening. Mark and his wife, Brenda, came Saturday morning, and they were also staying until Sunday evening. That made the count nine kids, including Brent as the lone 'friend', and eight adults would be there.

For dinner Anna had prepared a dozen gigantic salmon steaks and all the classics around them, including brown rice, fried rice and steamed rice plus a vegetable medley, several sauces, and a huge Caesar salad.

When everyone was seated, Russ raised his wine glass full of diet coke and declared, "To a great cook and a stunning meal and to a wonderful family that makes me happy to be a father and grandfather and to Lynn for … ah… just being Lynn, the best friend I could ever imagine and to Diana, Jay, and Brent who are probably hoping I will sit down quickly before all the food gets cold." He raised his glass, as did everyone else. Lots of glass clinking and laughter followed. Even Charlotte seemed happy.

Maybe a week on the Farm can really charm anyone…

The conversations were many and diverse. But every once in a while, someone commandeered the whole table. It was usually someone asking if they all remembered when… and that 'when' would be some event where Russ/Dad/GP had gotten them to go off on some ill-advised venture. Whether it was rafting the wrong section of the American River, the rainy week in Hawaii which may have been the most fun week ever, or the weekend he loaded all the kids into the car for breakfast at Hobee's only to tell them they were driving to Yosemite instead for two days of camping for which they were totally unprepared.

I loved listening to the stories. I realized the Farm was just an extension of a life that Russ had been living for a very long time.

First he adjusts to reality… then he just changes his view of reality… then he works to have everyone else view it the same way… and the result is… happy…maybe True Happiness…

Anna had outdone herself for dessert. She had two --
her warm triple thick fudge brownies with vanilla ice cream
on top, or her famous apple tart.

I ate too much of everything, but that did not stop me
from trying my hardest to beat Alex in air hockey. It was
hopeless. He just had faster reflexes than me… I needed to
adjust to reality. Dan's Dad, Mark, got a two-on-two
basketball game going with Brent and Dan. The eighteen-
year olds were too quick for us. Then Alex and Dan played
Brent and me. I lost again, and it was becoming painfully
obvious who the 'weak link' was. I joined a group
bowling….

The night in the game room went on until midnight
for me and later for Russ. I had committed to an early ride
the next day with Marci and Alicia…

I went up to the house for a quick breakfast, met
Marci and Alicia, and then head down to the stables. Marci's
mother, Brenda, joined us, and the girls wanted to race on the
beach. So that's what we did.

While the girls were racing in the surf, Brenda rode
up close to me. "Jay, I just wanted to say thanks for all the
time you spent with Marci this week. On the phone she kept
talking about 'Uncle Jay' and how much fun she was having
with you and Alicia."

"It was me having fun with them. When in my life would I have ever gone surf racing on a horse if it were not for the two of them?"

"I think you helped make it extra special for Marci. Alicia can be a bit intimidating. I saw an extra spark in Marci yesterday."

This is Dan's mother… Do I say anything to help here?… Remember she's not going to change unless she decides to change… But there's nothing to lose… so just do it.

"I think Marci and all your kids thrive here." I had her attention. "I really think part of it is Russ's 'no rules' system."

"Yes but…"

I didn't let her finish that negative thought. "Russ says that the 'no rules' is just an extension of his belief that if you set someone free, especially someone you love, they will respond by wanting to be with you more. If… they really love you."

I kept going, "I have seen it work well here on the Farm. All the grandkids always want to be with him. They are always asking advice of him. And basically, they are all teenagers, so it must be quite powerful to work on them.

Anyway I thought you might like an outsider's view of the one reason why they all enjoy being here so much."

Brenda heard me, but I am not sure she really 'heard me' if you know what I mean. But maybe… I think she did yelled fewer instructions to Marci on the rest of the ride.

We got back to the house in time for lunch, which was a buffet of all the week's leftovers. There were so many dishes I had liked during the past week I couldn't decide which ones to pick. I was the last one through the line, so I could take my time and ponder my choices.

The kids quickly filled their plates and went back to the game room to eat. Russ was sitting at the table with all the other adults except for me.

Just as I put the last meatball on my plate, Dan was standing in the hall with a basketball and inviting me for a game of one on one. Diana had chosen just that moment to come back to the counter and add more potato salad to her plate.

A bunch of thoughts entered my brain all at once… *spend time doing what makes you happy… it is okay to plan for the future… this is a type three decision, make it quick…*

With that, I spoke to Diana, but loud enough for Dan to hear, "Save me a piece of the pumpkin pie. I will need it after I whip Dan in a quick game." And then I headed off to the game room, hoping I had covered all the bases.

One game with Dan of course led to a second and then a third. Then, I looked around and saw Diana there holding a big piece of pumpkin pie.

"Want this?" she said. "It will cost you one game of Ms Pac-Man when you finish this game with Dan… deal?"

"Ah… yes." With this, I was totally distracted and Dan scored the next four points and I lost the tiebreaker game.

Then I got killed at Ms Pac-Man, but the pie was great and I was really happy Diana had brought it to me.

Two hours later everyone was saying goodbye at the front door. I have to admit that as much fun as the week had been, or maybe because it was so much fun, I was sad now thinking that this week might be the last one like this for Russ and his grandchildren. I knew Russ would flip that on me and tell me to be happy and feel lucky that I was able to be part of such a week. I thought I will be a happier person when I learn to accept reality and change my view of it…

18

Monday was a good work day, and Russ and I had made great progress on many of the documents and decisions that needed to be made.

The biggest and most complex work centered around the Farm itself. There were different ways to approach it, and Fenwick & West had presented several ideas to Russ to think about.

I noticed that Diana was taking more of the calls from the operating businesses and handling as much as she could, asking Russ only the few questions she could not answer. I was impressed. But then again I was 'impressed' when Diana said good morning to me in the office.

The Kelly/roommate debacle was fading, but I sensed it still had residual effects. 'Forgive, Forget, Move On' still took some time.

Russ and I were working on a problem with the Paris travel company when he started to explain another of his grand theories.

"Do you know the bell curve?" he asked.

"Sure," I said. "It is the graph curve that is highest in the middle and both ends get lower as each end moves away from the middle."

"Correct," he continued. "I think it's a great way to explain much of human behavior. Lots of people sit under the middle of the curve, but in either direction the number of people under the curve goes down."

"For example what is the height of most Americans? Turns out that for men, the midpoint is five feet nine inches. Of course, that is the most likely answer, but there are almost as many Americans at five feet eight inches and five feet ten inches. Still, as you go out in either direction, the number of people goes down, and at say six feet six inches and five feet, you don't find very many people at all."

"The same curve works on say ice cream flavors. Take vanilla for example. If you ask people to rate vanilla ice cream from 1 to 10, more people could give it a score of 7 than any other score. Scores of 6 and 8 would most likely be the next highest scores. You can see that this bell curve is not always symmetrical, since the high point is 7 which is obviously not in the middle. If you tested pistachio flavored ice cream, you might find its curve would look much different, but it would still be a bell curve."

"What I find most interesting is using the bell curve to find mistakes in perception. For example, is the most popular movie necessarily the best movie? Not according to the Academy Awards. The most popular movie seldom wins the Best Picture award. So, if you're trying to pick a movie to watch, the question is which bell curve do you want to be on? One curve is of all the ticket buyers in the world. The other is the curve of industry people who are voting members of the Academy of Motion Pictures. I guess the answer to that is about who you are…"

"If you get good at this analysis, you will constantly question the information you're fed. Yelp, Trip Advisor, Rotten Tomatoes, Facebook, Zagat, Michelin, etc. You'll ask 'what are they really telling me?' It depends on which bell curve you want to trust."

At this point my mind was just spinning. I think I am going to write about this in my notes tonight and see if I can figure it all out then.

Maybe I can get this one, maybe I can't…

But what I said was, "I think I've got it." It was a really weak response based on Farm language standards.

19

Tuesday was April 1st, April Fool's Day, and the joke was going to be on me.

The day started normally. I was in the kitchen by 8:30 and poured a bowl of cereal for breakfast and sliced some bananas on top. Nothing wrong there.

I went to my office, got a couple of projects done, and talked with Russ and Diana a bit. Lynn was up in San Francisco for a couple of days. Nothing wrong there either.

To try to finish some the new documents for the Farm, I had a 10:00 meeting with one of the partners in the cut-flower business. I drove my car down to the meeting, and it went very well. He signed off on the changes we needed. Nothing wrong there.

I drove back and came in through the main gate, as it was shorter time-wise. I saw a rental car parked in front of the house and wondered whose it might be. But, I drove down to my cottage, parked there, and walked back up to the house.

Anna and Diana were in the kitchen. Diana was eating a sandwich, and Anna was working on plans for dinner.

Her mouth was half full, so Diana pointed upstairs. "There's a surprise visitor waiting upstairs for you."

"Who?"

"You'll see." She pointed upstairs again.

My previous encounters with 'you'll see' had not been good, so I was starting to get a bit worried. I headed to the stairs and up to the entry.

The IRS with a surprise audit… no they don't have this address… someone to repossess my car… no I'm current… who could this be…

I reached the top of the stairs and seated there looking in my direction was Rachel. She was smiling shyly at me…

Rachel… holy shit… what is she doing here?… how did she get here… how…

I hadn't moved from the top of the stairs, so Rachel stood up and walked over to me and kissed me gently… on the lips.

We hadn't spoken a word yet. Then she said, "Sorry for the surprise, but when I decided to come out here, I wanted to talk to you in person not on the phone… So here I am." She smiled again.

No shit… here you are… but why???

"Ah… yes, I can see that…. But how did you get here?" I wanted to ask why, but I was able to suppress that obvious attack question.

"I flew and then rented a car."

"Yes, but how did you know where I was? We haven't talked in three months."

"Don't be mad at your mother, but I called her on Friday and begged her for your address. I told her not to tell you that I might come out."

What was my mother thinking?… doesn't she know this is like the worse thing for me?…

"Ah… Rachel, it's certainly a surprise."

"I just came to talk. That is all…" She paused and then said. "We could go have lunch. Is there a place near here?"

I was lost. My first impulse was to just get her out of the house… *and out of my life too.*

"There are a couple of places I have seen in La Honda. It's pretty close."

"That's fine," she moved toward the door.

I also started for the door and then stopped. I was so shook up I wasn't thinking straight.

"Ah… wait here. I need to go downstairs and tell them I'm heading out."

I went down the stairs and over to Diana and Anna. Before I could speak, Diana pointed at the stairs and said, "Are you going to introduce us?"

I turned around. Rachel had walked to the bottom of the stairs.

What the hell… can't she just listen… for once?

"Ah… sure," I waved Rachel over to the kitchen.

She came over with a big smile on her face and acted very calm and casual. On the other hand, I was feeling really tense and out of control.

"Rachel… this is Diana and Anna."

Rachel put out her hand to Diana. "Nice to meet you." They shook hands, but before Diana could respond, Rachel said, "I met Anna at the door when I first got here."

It was a slight put down of Diana. I felt it, I hoped Diana hadn't.

Diana gets everything… of course she'll feel the put down…

"Ah… I'm going to go lunch with Rachel. I'll be back in a… a couple of hours." Rachel had already turned and headed toward the stairs.

If she didn't really want to meet them, why did she come down the stairs… just to put them down???

We went out the front door.

"Is La Honda near the ocean?"

"No, it's up the hill."

"Oh. Is there another place near the ocean? I've never been to the Pacific Ocean."

"The only place I know is the General Store in San Gregorio. It has sandwiches. But it isn't fancy."

"Let's do that."

She walked to the driver's side of her car and said, "I'll drive. You can navigate."

Was she always this controlling?

"Okay."

And was I always such a wuss?...

Even though San Gregorio was only about seven miles from the house, there was no short route to get there. It took us nearly twenty minutes. Most of that time she talked about her flight and the problems she had finding the house and then getting Anna to let her through the gate.

"Finally, I just said I was your girlfriend."

I know that Diana knows my story, but does Anna? I wonder what Anna is thinking?… I can fix that later…

"I bet that surprised her." I had to say something, and it was the best I could do.

"I don't know, but she opened the gate, and that was all I wanted."

Callous… not caring…

When we pulled up in front of the General Store, Rachel noted, "This place is a dump. Is the food safe?"

"Yes, I've eaten here a couple of times, and the sandwiches are quite good."

And a snob… what ever captivated me?

Well, I soon found out.

We sat at a small table in the store. The sandwiches were excellent as 'advertised'. Rachel ordered wine for herself and 'insisted' on ordering a beer for me.

She told me how stupid she felt and that she had made the biggest mistake in her life. She said she had come to beg for a second chance. That we had so much going on together. She wanted us to start fresh when I got back to Chicago.

But it wasn't the words she was saying that got to me. It was the way she held her body, the inviting way she caressed me with her eyes. It was the same physical attraction that I had felt for four years. She still had all of that.

Our lunch lasted over an hour with all the talking…

"Can you show me the beach here?" Rachel was at her flirtatious best.

"Ah… Okay. There is a nice state beach right here. It's less than a mile."

We drove down to the beach. It had a parking lot right next to it. The day was sunny, but since it was a Tuesday in early April, no one else was parked in the lot, and no one was on the beach.

We got out of the car and walked out onto the sand. The waves were rolling in and crashing about twenty yards from where we were standing. If you've not seen bigger waves, they are impressive.

"Jay… this is really spectacular." She took her shoes off and ran to the edge of the water. "Oh… this water is cold." She ran down the beach, and I watched. It brought back memories of our vacations to the Bahamas and St. Croix. It was hard for me not to feel the pull

.

She came running back and grabbed my hand. "Walk me down the beach." She pulled me forward. We walked for a bit in silence with her bouncing into me more than was necessary.

What the hell am I doing here???

"What's that?" she pointed at a cave in the cliff wall very near where we were walking. She ran toward it and waved at me to join her.

We had walked into the cave only about five feet when she turned and kissed me. Kissed me passionately like she had for the past four years. And I… I kissed her back.

She kept kissing me and pushed me down hard enough to push me to the sand with her on top of me. It felt great. It felt like I remembered. I was losing my grip on everything.

What the hell am I doing??

Then I snapped back to the present. And reality

What the 'hell' am I doing… this is a huge mistake… this is not what I want in my life…

I stopped kissing her and rolled her off of me. I stood up quickly and looked down at her. "This is not right… we are not right… we are over, and I think it should stay that way."

She sat there stunned and silent for a minute. Then she spoke with a touch of anger. "What did you say?"

"I said that this was not right. You and I are not right for each other."

"I told you I made a mistake. I told you I was sorry. What more do you want?" Despite the words I still heard a bit of anger in her voice. She stood up.

"Rachel. You're not listening to me. It's not about the past. It's about now and the future. We are not right for each other."

"What are you talking about? We were engaged to be married. You said you loved me more than anything in the world. What happened to all that?"

"No... I meant all that when I said it, but being here has helped me to figure out who I am and what I want to do with my life. I don't think you and I are right for each other anymore."

"Oh... so you come out to California, and now you're a different person. I don't think so. I think it's that young girl I saw in the kitchen. Are you hooked up with her already?"

I wanted to hit her, but I didn't... I just turned and walked out of the cave and down the beach.

"That's it, isn't it? You're just like me. You jumped in the next bed you could find."

I wished I could shut her up.

"No, I am not sleeping with Diana. But I can tell you one thing. She would be much better for me than you are."

"You little shit. How dare you say that to me after our four years together."

This is nuts…

"Four years together didn't seem to stop you with Craig." Craig was my old boss at the Chicago law firm whom she had the affair with.

She stood there with her mouth open. Then she shut it, didn't say another word, and walked quickly up the beach toward the parking lot. I stood there watching her, relieved that I didn't have to talk to her anymore.

I saw her pick up her shoes and go to the car. She got in and drove off. And after a minute or two, I walked up the beach as well. I walked slowly. I was exhausted from all the emotion I felt.

When I got to the parking lot, I realized I didn't have my cell phone with me. I walked the half mile back to the General Store and asked if I could borrow their phone. I called Diana and told her I had a fight with Rachel and I was stuck at the General Store. Could she come pick me up?

About twenty minutes later, Diana pulled up in her Mini in front of the store. I stood up to get into her car, but she hopped out. "Let me buy you a beer. I think you need one."

I nodded. As I turned to go back inside I asked, "Do I look that bad?"

Now Diana was looking at my back she said, "Yes, you do, and given how much sand is on the back of your pants, I'm guessing there's quite a story."

I had totally forgotten about that. I tried to dust some of the sand off, but really, it was too late...

We went in, Diana bought us two beers and we sat at a table, a different table than I had sat with Rachel. The bartender must have wondered a bit about what I was up to. But, I am sure, like most bartenders, he had seen much stranger things than this.

I told Diana the whole story, all of it including my feelings. It felt good to tell someone. And I felt better afterward.

"Russ would be proud of you."

"For dumping Rachel?"

"Ah... yes, but much more for getting your thoughts in the right order."

"What do you mean by the right order?"

"Do you remember Russ talking about this with Lynn a couple of weeks ago? Basically, he says that there are two big questions in life. Where are you going in your life? And who will go with you? The trick is to get the two in the right order. Too many people find a mate and then figure out where they are going and end up with the wrong person because of it."

"Yeah… but at this point, I'm not sure I have any idea where I want to go."

"Good reason not to be picking out a wife then…" She smiled and toasted me with her beer.

I laughed. This girl was way ahead of me… again. Maybe it was two years with Russ versus my two months…

She drove me back to my cottage where I showered and changed for dinner. Nothing was said about my visitor. I'm not sure why, but I sure didn't bring it up.

Russ did say that tomorrow he would be at the lawyers until early afternoon. I knew they had finished two of the key documents the Will and the Trust, and he was probably going in to sign them.

Alicia reminded me that tomorrow was Wednesday, a short day, and she was hoping I was going riding with her again. I confirmed I was.

20

Wednesday morning was a good one for me. I got a major agreement completed with the partners in Russ's online marketplace company. It had been a sticky process, and I was pleased to have everyone finally agree to the changes that would be necessary once Russ was no longer around.

When I thought about Russ 'not being around', I still got tense, but less so. He was teaching me not to let anything from the past or the future 'ruin' my today. Just watching him, I was learning a lot…

Alicia made a snack for us as usual, and we rode out to the lake. She was in especially good spirits as she and Bronco had just jumped the higher rails for the first time. Of course she asked me her usual questions. This time Rachel came up. She had heard a 'rumor' that Rachel had shown up at the house, and I had sent her back to Chicago.

I gave her a more accurate account. I thought it might help her someday. I also told her about getting the two questions in the right order. Then she said.

"Oh… I know that one already. It could be a long time before I know where I am going with my life."

"You're twelve. I think you have lots of time for that."

She gave Bronco some extra carrots to reward him for the good jumps and got back on. I loved the way they interacted with each other.

When we got back to the stable, Alicia asked if I would wait at the jumping arena while she did one more round with Bronco. She had never done this before at the end of a ride, but I agreed. We had plenty of time.

She was doing fine until the final hurtle. Bronco hit the top rail with one of his front hooves. It looked like they would be all right, but when they landed, Bronco buckled and went down and Alicia was thrown over the front. Neither of them moved right away. I jumped off Chestnut and went running to where they were.

"Alicia, are you okay?" I yelled.

No answer.

"Alicia!" I yelled again louder.

Still no answer. However, as I got closer, I could see her starting her to move. I knelt down next to her and told her to lie still. I knew that if she had any serious injury moving could make it worse.

"I think I'm okay," she said.

I didn't know exactly what to do, so I asked her to slowly move her hands and feet first. Then her arms and legs. Finally, I asked if she could move her head. They all seemed fine. So we slowly stood up. I was thinking it was lucky she had her riding helmet on, and then I heard her scream.

"Bronco!"

I had been so focused on Alicia I hadn't noticed that Bronco was still on the ground. When he tried to get up, his right leg seemed to hurt too much for him to use it.

Alicia was immediately next to him, talking to him and stroking his head.

"It's going to be all right, Bronco. I'm here. Everything is going to be all right." As it always did, her voice calmed Bronco down and he lay still with her.

I told her I would run to get Harry.

She said, "Call GP."

I did both. Russ answered as I was getting close to the stable.

"Jay?"

"Hi Russ. We have a problem down here at the stables. Alicia missed a jump. She's okay, but Bronco is having trouble standing."

"I'll be right down. Does Harry know?"

"I'm looking for him now."

"Okay. He will know what to do."

I walked into the stable and saw one of the stable hands.

"Do you know where Harry is?"

"Ah… yeah. I think he's in the house."

"Thanks." I walked quickly over to the white farm house. The door was open with only the screen door closed. I yelled, 'Harry' as I entered.

"I'm in the kitchen."

I went back there and found him working on a small piece of equipment in the sink. I explained what had happened, and we both went running back to the jumping arena.

Bronco and Alicia had not moved. She was still stroking his head and talking to him as we approached.

Bronco's eyes looked a bit tense as Harry took a closer look. He took out his cell phone, "I'm calling Doc Hopkins." He stepped away from us.

I spoke to Alicia, "How is he doing?"

"He seems frightened, but as long as I keep talking to him he's staying calm."

I decided to sit down next to Alicia. I had no idea what to do to help, but I decided getting Harry and calling Russ were the best things I could have done.

Harry came back. "Doc said he can be here in twenty minutes."

Alicia turned to Bronco. "Hear that? The doctor is coming in twenty minutes. He will make it better and give you some medicine so it doesn't hurt so bad."

By now I knew that Bronco may have broken his leg. I had no idea how serious that was, but I knew that in the old days it was fatal, and they usually shot the horse so that it would not suffer.

With better medicine today did they still have to do that?

It was only a couple of minutes later that Russ showed up. He drove his pickup right up to the jumping arena and hopped out.

Harry walked over to the truck and talked to Russ before they approached us.

Before he could say anything Alicia burst out. "GP, it's all my fault. If I hadn't wanted one more jump, none of this would've happened."

"Pumpkin. Bronco loves jumping with you. It's his favorite thing to do. It's not your fault. Accidents happen."

She stroked Bronco's head a few times and then looked up at Russ. "It's serious, isn't it?"

Russ looked her right in the eyes. "Yes it is. We will have to wait for the vet to get here before we really know how serious it is. For right now you are doing a great job of keeping Bronco calm so that he does not try to get up and have more pain."

I just sat next to Alicia as she attended to Bronco. The care in her voice was tremendous. You could physically feel her love for Bronco.

In a short time, Doc Hopkins pulled up in his truck. Both Russ and Harry met him before he came over to us. With a name like 'Doc Hopkins' I was expecting a white haired vet. But he was more like mid-forties.

He bent over and shook my hand. "Hi, I'm Bill Hopkins". Then he turned to Alicia and said. "You must be Alicia and this is your horse Bronco."

She came right to the point. "Can you fix him?"

"That's what I'm here to figure out. Now I'm going to examine Bronco, and you just keep talking to him. It should help. But if I hit the wrong spot, it may hurt him a bit. So if he moves quickly, be prepared to move out of his way a bit."

"Okay," she said and went back to talking to Bronco and stoking his head. "The doctor is here, and he needs to look at you to see how to fix you. So you can just lie still with me."

Doc Hopkins went to work looking at all parts of Bronco, but mainly his two front legs. It was then that I noticed that not only was the right leg injured, but the left leg may have been injured even more. A small pool of blood was under it near the knee joint.

Bronco only moved twice during the examination. The doctor took his time and spent twenty to thirty minutes looking closely at Bronco. Time was hard to keep track of, given all the emotions we were feeling. A couple of times he pushed a sensitive spot and bronco jerked, but never tried to bolt

After his examination, he stood up and walked away with Russ and Harry to talk to them.

Then Russ came back to us. He knelt down close to Alicia.

"It's not good news. Bronco broke both of his front legs and his left leg is shattered and complicated by a compound fracture which is why he is bleeding a little bit."

"What does that mean?"

What a girl... She asks the tough questions first...

"It means we are going to lose Bronco. He can't stand up with two broken legs, and if he stays on his side he will die in a few days. If we let that happen, it will be very painful for Bronco."

Alicia didn't cry out loud, but tears started to come down her cheeks. She just stroked Bronco's head silently. Then she looked back at Russ.

"When?"

Russ didn't seem to understand. So Alicia repeated her question.

"When do we lose him?"

"Soon. Doc Hopkins is preparing medicine that will put Bronco to sleep, so he won't be in pain anymore."

"And he dies in his sleep?"

"Yes."

She continued to stroke Bronco and went back to talking to him. "The doctor is making some medicine for you. It will put you asleep, and you won't hurt anymore." The tears continued flowing down her cheeks

A few minutes later the doctor came with a needle connected to a sack of liquid.

Russ said to Alicia. "It's time now. Is there anything you want to tell Bronco?"

Alicia didn't look up but continued to stroke Bronco. "You're my best friend. You know that, don't you? I love you more than anything else in this world. You have been a great friend to me all these years."

While Alicia was focused on Bronco's face and talking to him, Doc Hopkins started the injection.

Alicia kept talking and stroking her friend. "You taught me all I know about horses and riding. Did you know that? You did. And you will always be my best friend for the rest of my life. And after I die, I will see you in Heaven."

As she continued to talk, Bronco's eyes slowly closed, and as they did I noticed Alicia's face starting to break into a true cry. But Bronco kept breathing even after his eyes closed. She kept talking to him.

After a bit, it was hard to tell if he was breathing. Doc Hopkins put his stethoscope on and listened to Bronco's heart. He gave a sign to Russ, who leaned back toward us.

He put his hand on Alicia's shoulder. "He's gone."

She didn't move. She stopped stroking his head, but didn't move. She sat there for a minute or two and then looked at me. She hugged me as hard as she could. And I just held her . Her tears ran down her cheeks and onto my shirt.

After a couple of minutes, she let go and asked, "Can you take me back to the house?"

"Yes, of course."

I started to get up and saw Alicia look at GP. "Is it okay if Uncle Jay takes me back?"

Russ said, "Sure. I will be here with Harry for a while."

Alicia and I walked down to the golf cart. I hadn't noticed, but someone had taken Chestnut into the stable and brushed her down, so we could go ahead and drive home.

We didn't say much on the ride. Alicia just hung onto my arm. One thing she did say was, "If only I hadn't asked him to do one more jump."

I told her it wasn't her fault, that it was an accident. Despite that, she said the same thing two or three more times.

When we got to the house, she thanked me for helping. Then she went to her room and said she would be skipping dinner.

It was already 8:00 when I got to my cottage. I showered and changed clothes and walked back up to the house. I was pretty shaken.

If I am shaken, I wonder what Alicia is feeling...

Then I remembered my childhood dog. Her name was 'Dollar'. Dollar was five, and I was fourteen when she died from eating a sharp chicken bone. It made me sad all over again now just remembering that day.

Anna had just put out leftovers for anyone to take and heat up as they wanted. No one else was in the kitchen when I came in. Anna came in from the supply room and hugged me. I asked her if Alicia had come out. She said 'no', but Russ was with her. He had taken her a chicken sandwich and some milk.

I was actually the last to eat. Diana had eaten with Alex and Kevin, and then they had gone to their rooms immediately. I wasn't very hungry, so I decided a chicken sandwich sounded best. I made it and asked Anna if she minded if I took it back to my room to eat.

I tried to write in my journal, but I couldn't focus… it was the same when I tried finishing my second Dick Francis book. My mind kept picturing Bronco closing his eyes while Alicia stroked his head.

What a brave little girl… she held it together better than I could, even today… I hope she's getting some comfort from Russ.

Finally, I decided to go to bed. I tried reading the book again, but luckily I was so tired from the tough day, I fell fast asleep.

21

In the morning, I found out from Anna that Alicia had gone to school. Russ had decided to drive them. I went up to my office, and by 9:30 Russ was back.

Today we were going to finalize how to handle the Farm. The documents were lengthy, and there was a very long list of decisions to make. Mainly, how to best preserve the Farm for both the family and eventually the public in general, minimize any tax issues, and not have it all become a burden on the family after Russ was gone.

One problem to address was that the Farm was by far the most valuable 'asset' Russ owned. It was hard to guess the value, but it was more than $10 million and probably less than $25 million. No private land tract this big existed in the county, so trying to figure a precise value was nearly impossible.

Russ wanted the family to enjoy the Farm as long as they wanted to and if they didn't want it anymore, he wanted it opened to the public.

The good news was that taken together the cut-flower and artichoke operations made enough money to pay for all the costs of the property. The largest cost was the real estate property taxes each year.

Fenwick & West had done an excellent job in figuring out everything the way Russ wanted it. But still, he and I needed to review the plan one more time.

"Sometimes I feel like I should just sell the Farm."

"What? You love this place," I said.

"I meant after I die. One of my keys to happiness is making sure you 'own' your possessions, rather than having them 'owning' you."

"What does that mean?" I asked. I was pleased that I was learning how to ask the simple questions if I didn't understand something.

He continued, "I'm sure you've seen people who keep jobs they hate just to support a house that is bigger than they can afford. Or a vacation house they go to all the time, not because they want to, but because they own it and think they have to use it a lot to get their money's worth from it. Or even the fancy car they park five rows from anyone else in a parking lot to protect it and walk from there."

"Their lives are being run by the things they own... What I like about my pickup truck is that it's paid for and if someone bangs it in a parking lot, I might not even notice. I am not saying never have nice things around, just don't let them 'own' you."

I did understand his point. "Yeah, some of my classmates from law school have already bought the fancy Mercedes and the water view condo. They have such high payments on them they can never quit the treadmill. I understand not wanting to get into that situation. "

Russ responded, "Yes, but it's a slippery slope. It can be cool vacations or a girlfriend who spends money like water and you are enchanted. There are lots of ways to get in over your head. That is why I want to make sure this Farm never does that to anyone. Since the Farm started as a luxury for me, I tried to pay cash for everything I've built here. If I didn't have enough money, then I waited. Those decisions have allowed me to enjoy the Farm without it ever becoming a rock around my neck."

We talked more about the Farm and in the end went through the entire set of agreements to make sure they all did what he wanted. They had. Russ called the lawyers to say he would be in their offices on Friday to sign the finalized versions. With that accomplished, he said we needed a couple of games of air hockey to relax.

The kids all had after school events and Diana was scheduled to pick them up. She ended up taking them to

Buck's for dinner, and they got back when Russ, Anna and I were finishing dinner. They came down to say hello, but only Alex stayed for dessert. Kevin and Alicia went straight to their rooms.

Alex was learning how to play chess. I am not good at chess, but I do know the rules. We found an old plastic set and sat by the fireplace and played. It had been foggy all day, and the fog along with the fire made it feel like a good time to play a game like chess.

I asked Alex how he felt Alicia was doing.

"She is trying not to show it, but I think she is still very sad. And she still feels like it was her fault."

We talked a bit more about Alicia as we played. I was thinking I wanted to see if somehow I could comfort her tomorrow.

22

Friday morning, I came into the kitchen. Only Diana was there sitting at the counter with a bowl of cereal in front of her. She was looking sad. I assumed she was still feeling the overall sadness from Alicia losing Bronco, but it turned out to be something else.

I came up next to her and said quietly, "Morning Diana."

She looked up, and I could see she had been crying, "Oh, hi." She looked back down at the counter.

I sat on the stool next to her and asked, "Are you still feeling sad about Bronco?"

She looked at me and started crying softly, "No… it's Russ."

I wondered exactly what happened.

Did Russ have another attack… no she would not be here like this, and someone would have told me… what is it?… ah… I know… Russ told her…

I gave her a hug. "I know. It's very sad. Did he just tell you?"

"No, he told me last night. I couldn't sleep. He said you and Lynn know, but no one else… How could this be true?"

Diana was where I was just a month ago, in disbelief. I had great empathy for her and her feelings. The idea of Russ being gone was hard to take. I knew she was planning on spending lots of time with him, even while she was in graduate school.

Finally, I said, "I agree. It's totally unfair. Unfair to Russ and everyone around him. I spent a week trying to figure it all out. Eventually, I did what Russ told me to do. Accept reality and don't let anything in the future ruin my life today. I took my lead from him."

"That is easier to say than do right now," was all she said.

I had no response that didn't sound condescending… So I said nothing. I got up. Got myself a bowl of Raisin Bran with milk and came back and sat down next to her in silence, hoping that she wanted me there with her right now.

I got my answer immediately. She turned and hugged me and cried for a bit. Finally, she let go and said, "Russ said he didn't want a bunch of sad people around him. The least I can do for him is not sit here and cry." With that she put a spoonful of her cereal in her mouth and slowly starting chewing.

We ate in silence for a couple of minutes. Then she said, "I have a Paris call in five minutes, so I'm going to finish this in my office. And thanks...thanks for letting me cry."

As if I could stop her...

The only thing I could think of saying was 'anytime'... Thank goodness I just kept my mouth shut and didn't say something really stupid.

I finished my cereal, went to my office and tried to work. But Diana's sadness was causing the same in me. Then I thought.

This is exactly what Russ is worried about. A bunch of sad people ruining his last days... he wants to enjoy those days as much as he can. I need to break out of this mood...

I left my office and went to the game room. I knew what to do. I went directly to the Ms. Pac-Man game, turned it on, and started to play. Within ten minutes all I was thinking about was the game. Ten minutes later I was happily playing the game.

I finally stopped and thought about Russ teaching me to have fun for a part of every day. He said I would be happier. It worked. Even though I was still thinking about him, I was no longer sad, but instead marveling at all he had taught me in only six weeks.

Lunchtime came. I leaned into Diana's office and asked her if she wanted to join me. She said 'yes', and we went down to the kitchen. It was still empty. Anna was doing shopping and waiting to bring the kids home from school.

We made our sandwiches, and Diana said, "You know, one thing bothers me. I had planned the next two years to have Russ still in my life. Now I'll never have that. I know you're right to enjoy the time with him I have now, but it's still hard to give up my imagined future."

I know… I have been learning to do a lot of that this year… And then there is John Lennon's song…

A smile crossed my face and I almost laughed.

"What's funny?" she asked.

"Oh I was just thinking of what Russ told me last week, when I was complaining about a change of plans we had to make. He said his favorite quote from a song was John Lennon's, 'Life is what happens to you while you're busy making other plans.' He told me that keeping that song in mind helped him when everything kept changing no matter what he was planning on."

Diana thought for a minute and then looked sad again. "I'm really going to miss all his non-stop wisdoms…"

"Me too. Actually, I've been writing them down."

"You have?"

"I don't know exactly why, but Russ said something on the first day I was here that I really wanted to remember, so I wrote it in my journal that night. I have been doing that almost every night since. Occasionally, I go back and read them again. Amazing insights…"

We talked a bit more. She started to relax and even laugh at some of the stories she told about Russ and some of the phone calls she had been on with him. She said he was a master at asking the toughest questions with a sense of humor.

We finished eating, and I suggested that we take a walk to what everyone always called 'the Far Veranda'. I am not sure where the name came from. It was neither a veranda nor that far away. It was a view point with a large covered deck built on it only about a quarter mile from the house.

Part of the path to the Far Veranda was a bit of a climb, almost straight up in some places. The view there included the coastline and some of Half Moon Bay. The deck had heat lamps, a barbeque, and my favorite, a pair of telescopes. I could even watch surfers from up there.

We walked up to it and sat for a minute on the benches near the edge which gave the best views.

Diana said, "When I came up here with Russ the first time, we sat right here. He told me he liked to come here when something was going poorly. He said he would sit and look out at the view and think 'Things could be a whole hell of a lot worse.' "

Diana continued, "He is right. To think I can sit here and enjoy this spectacular view in the middle of a workday... it's a good way to spend some time."

While she was talking I was thinking. *Somehow she has become 'important' to me... I can't explain it, but I can feel it... I want her to do well... to feel happy...*

We stayed in that amazing spot for a little while. Luckily I had been smart enough to grab a couple of Anna's super-sized chocolate chip cookies from the kitchen and put them in my pocket.

I pulled one out. "Cookie for your thoughts."

She grabbed the cookie out of my hand, smiled at me and said, "I think I'll just keep this thought to myself." She then took a big bite of the cookie.

What a mix of emotions was running through me. I was intrigued by Diana, sad about Russ, and sad about Alicia and Bronco.

I never realized how much was going on around me before... has it always been this way, but here on this farm I am learning to see it… or are these just special circumstances and soon life will go back in the 'bottle' where I have been keeping it all these years…

Diana finally said, "Thanks for this idea. I do feel better now. I think I need to get back. I want to finish one project before the weekend."

23

On Saturday I found myself on a long walk with Alicia. At dinner on Friday, she had asked if we could walk Saturday morning instead of riding. Of course, I said 'yes'. At 10:00, I met her in the kitchen. She had made lunch just like all the other Saturdays, except this time she had a small backpack to put it in.

When she saw me she all she said was, "Ready?"

"Sure." We went the kitchen door and headed out on the trail that I knew led to the Far Veranda. So I asked.

"Where are we headed?"

"Margie's Peak."

"Okay."

I wasn't exactly sure how far it was to Margie's Peak from the house. I had only ridden up there from the stable. It turned out to be a couple of miles with lots of ups and downs on the trail as it wound over and around the hills and into the forest. Alicia kept up a good pace, so I was starting to sweat a bit. Unlike our rides, Alicia was not a chatterbox. I assumed it was because she was still grieving for Bronco.

After about an hour, she stopped for a water break. She asked me how I was doing and noted how much harder it was to get there walking rather than riding. She was still the 'take charge' girl. We eventually got to Margie's Peak where we sat down at the picnic table that had a great view. The sun had come up since the last water break, and I was getting a bit dehydrated. I had my own water, so I took it out and offered her some.

"No. I'll just have some of my own. Let's have lunch now, Okay?" She was already unpacking her backpack.

"Sounds good."

She had brought more food than usual. Two sandwiches each, a couple of apples, a big bad of chips and four of the super-sized chocolate chip cookies. I guess she assumed hiking would make us hungry. In my case, she was right.

After eating for a minute in silence, Alicia asked, "Do you remember coming here on our first ride?"

"Yes, of course. It was fun to follow you up the mountain."

"I wanted to come here because it was my favorite place to ride with Bronco. I think he liked it too. I always gave him extra carrots because of how steep it was. And…"

"I just miss him," and she started to cry.

I didn't know what to do. *Should I get up and sit next to her and console her… or is she alright??*

She stopped crying for a second. "You know he was my best friend," and then she cried some more.

I got up and went to sit next to her. Not touching her, just next to her. She stopped crying again and looked at me, "You know what it's like to lose your best friend."

I didn't have to think hard for my response, "Yes I do, and it hurts."

"Did you cry when Rachel left you?"

"Yes, I did."

"How long did it hurt?"

"It hurt until last week when I saw her again and realized she was not the right person for me to have as a friend."

"Oh…" I think she realized that her hurt for Bronco was very different.

I had had an idea about Alicia and Bronco yesterday. I reached for my wallet, and I pulled out a twenty-year-old photo. It was picture of a small black dog, about the size of a beagle, but it had the look of a small black Labrador. I handed Alicia the photo. "This is a picture of Dollar. She was my dog from when I was ten."

"What kind of dog is she?" Alicia asked.

"Just a mutt. We got her at the dog pound after I had begged my Mom for years to get a dog. She was my dog, and I paid a dollar to buy her at the pound. That's where I came up with the idea for her name.

"I didn't realize it, until I came here and watched you with Bronco and listened to Russ about having one true friend that Dollar was my best friend for five years."

"When I was in school, I was a bit of a geek, and I didn't have lots of friends. But every day when I came home from school, Dollar would be standing in our driveway waiting for me. My mother had trained Dollar not to leave our yard, so she would jump up and down and bark when she saw me. It was a greeting that always made me feel special."

"What happened after those five years?"

"Apparently she ate a sharp chicken bone or something like that, and it killed her."

"Were you sad?"

"Just like you… I even miss her today…" I felt a small pang of sadness. "But mostly I just remember all the fun times we had together. I guess she was part Labrador and so she loved to play fetch with a ball. She would chase the ball for what seemed like hours. I would get tired of throwing it before she got tired of chasing it."

I felt better the more I talked about Dollar. I think Alicia sensed that.

"What did you do for a best friend after that?"

What did I do?...

"After a couple of months, we got another dog, but it wasn't the same. I think I was older then and had less time to spend time with our new dog. I ended up having a high school friend named Warren. He was a great friend for me. Still is, but he moved to London, so I don't get to see or talk to him too often."

"Ah… I think it's too soon to think about another horse. But, maybe my next best friend will not be a horse. Bronco was just special to me."

We sat together in silence for a minute. She took another bite of her sandwich. I pulled my second sandwich from the other side of the table and started to eat it. At one point, she hugged my arm like twelve-year old girls will do.

"Thanks for coming here with me. I needed to be here for Bronco."

I didn't say anything. I looked at Alicia. She was just staring out at the coastline. I think she was just remembering being here with Bronco.

We eventually finished our lunch, and Alicia was starting to feel better… I think. In any case she was full of questions again as usual.

When we got back to the house, I saw Russ reading by the fireplace, and I went to say hi. It turned out he was waiting to talk to me.

"Hey Jay. How was your walk with Alicia?"

I told him all I could remember and even showed him my photo of Dollar. He seemed pleased to hear the story.

"I'm glad you were able to do all that with Alicia. I think she has suffered a severe tragedy. She lost her main activity, her best friend, and she feels totally guilty about it."

"Yes," I said, "Alex told me last night she was still feeling guilty. I did not get much sense of that on our walk though."

Russ said, "I talked to her last night as best as I could. It is hard not to feel guilty when you are in the middle of grieving."

"In the end, I told her the story about how her grandmother died. I had planned a family ski vacation in Tahoe. The kids and I got there on a Thursday, but Margie had work to do and could not come until Friday after work. She was not going to come until I found some friends who were flying up in their private plane and they offered Margie a ride. I had the car, so she could come back with me and the kids."

"Margie was not a good skier and really only came to be supportive. Well, the plane crashed on landing. The pilot and Margie died in the crash."

"I blamed myself for a long time for pushing her to join us. I had to 'learn' that it wasn't my fault they crashed and that even if I contributed to her death, I had to forgive myself. Feeling guilty was making my life miserable and the kids' lives miserable too. Forgive, Forget, but definitely Move On. I have never told any of the grandchildren the story of their grandmother's death until now. I think Alicia understood that I felt just like she does now. I hope it helped her."

"As I said, she did seem better today than before, still sad, but able to talk a bit."

"Good. There's one more thing I would like you to consider."

"What is that?" I asked.

"My daughter, Katlin, called two days ago from Saigon. She confirmed that she and Andrew have been given an opportunity to add Tibet and Mongolia to their study. Apparently, this is a big deal to the World Bank. The problem is that they will not get back in the U.S. until late

June… Now that is okay here. Even though Lynn and I leave at the end of April for our big trip, Anna and Diana will be here. And that should work."

"I know that you and I will have almost everything completed in the next two to three weeks, but I would like to ask if you could stay on for two extra months. The kids have bonded quite a bit with you, especially Alicia."

"In addition, I know that Fenwick & West has been impressed with your work with them. So you wouldn't get bored if you stay. I asked Mark if they had any interesting projects you could help them with during that time. Mark thought it was an excellent idea and said they have a couple projects you could choose from."

"Anyway, I didn't know what your immediate plans were, so I thought I would make this offer. And, of course, there is always extra stuff you could do for me and the Farm."

No wonder he gets things done his way… he has this plan thought through before even mentioning it to me…

"Yes." I said.

"What? Did you just say 'yes'?" He smiled.

"Yes I did. I was just starting to think of what to do when I finished this visit. And giving me two more months to make any decisions sounds good."

Russ stuck out his hand, "Deal?"

"Deal." And I shook his hand.

Wow… two more months here… I think it's just what I need…

I went to bed that night a happy guy.

24

The next week was uneventful compared with the previous week, at least that is until Friday night.

During the week, Russ and I finished up almost all the paperwork for every venture. We only had a few items left to complete.

We did have an interesting conversation with his partner Pierre in Paris. I was explaining one of the paragraphs to him on the speaker phone with Russ sitting next to me when Pierre suddenly asked,

"Russ, how sick are you?"

Where did that come from?

Pierre kept going, "Are you dying?"

Nailed it…

I stayed silent.

Russ took a moment, and then answered, "I should have known you would eventually figure it all out. I personally thought you would have two weeks ago when Jay sent you the first draft."

"I did figure it out then. As a polite Frenchman, I chose not to say anything, but today I just had to. How are you feeling? Is it your old pancreas, or is it something new?"

I smiled. Pierre and Russ traded French and U.S. culture jokes during most of their conversations. And now Pierre was treating Russ's illness the way Russ wanted, like just another event to be dealt with. Obviously, they shared a lot in common.

"It's the pancreas. After twenty years of remission, it has decided to come back and bother me again."

"And right now, how do you feel?"

"Right now... I feel fine. I have had a couple of mild attacks, but nothing serious yet. With any luck, you'll have a couple more years of misery left dealing with me. By the way, do Thomas and Bertrand know?"

"I haven't said anything."

"Okay. I was planning on telling you when Lynn and I get to Paris in June. But there's no harm in them knowing now as long as you don't let them dwell on it."

"No problem here. But when you get to Paris, I do not want to hear about you playing it safe on going out to eat. It's not our rich French food that's killing you."

They both laughed.

I was thinking how with each of his partners Russ had been able to build a good personal bond. Each bond was different, but each was special. It was a trait I thought I'd like to try and emulate.

During the week, Russ had been his usual self with wisdom and fun. We were playing air hockey on Friday afternoon and after I beat him (again) he said.

"I know people often say life and sports are a lot alike. I think you can learn some good lessons from sports, but I think life and sports are very different. To me, life is not a contest. It's not something to win, to keep score with, or use to compare your life with others. Your life is to be savored like traveling down a slow moving river. All you need to be happy is to know that you tried your best to utilize the time and gifts that God gave you. Do that, and you will be happier than 90% of the Fortune 500 CEOs. Maybe happier than all of them." He laughed.

Then he continued, "Don't let your goals ruin your life. I watched some of my college classmates set goals and expectations for their lives. Then they proceeded to make choices and sacrifices based on those goals and expectations. I think too many of them gave up too much to reach those goals."

"I think our culture, especially the U.S. culture, is tilted too much in the direction of goals and progress… and money. It's too easy to get caught up with it when you talk with your friends and co-workers. We talk of new cars, big houses, and fancy resort vacations. My advice would be to balance reaching your goals with trying to enjoy life every day. Remember to have fun…"

Yes Russ… I will remember…

Friday night's dinner was one of my favorites -- Anna's spaghetti and meatballs.

It was Anna's turn at Word and she asked for Lynn and Russ to describe their upcoming trip. They both smiled and started right in. Half the time they both spoke at the same time. They were so excited.

They were starting in Tokyo visiting an old sports event partner of Russ's. The main feature there was going to their favorite breakfast sushi restaurant near the giant Tokyo Fish Market.

"Breakfast sushi, yuck," was Kevin's comment.

From there, they were going to Ulan Bator, Mongolia. Neither of them had been Mongolia before, but they were meeting Katlin and her husband there and spending a week with them. Then they were flying down to Xian, China, to see the terracotta soldiers, which Russ had wanted to see.

After Xian, they were meeting friends in Hong Kong. Apparently, they had been there several times, and Lynn was always in heaven with Tina, her 'shopping buddy.' Russ was a notoriously poor shopper.

While it was a long flight they had decided on visiting Lynn's college roommate who lived in Sydney. And from there they were flying to Mumbai for just three days. Russ had some old Indian partners there, and they had insisted he and Lynn stop in for a couple of days.

Then it was two weeks in Italy. A week at the Sirenuse in Positano, which Lynn said was her favorite romantic hotel in Italy. Lynn said, "Just walking down to Chez Black to have a pizza is all I need."

Plus they would spend a week at the Villa d'Este on Lake Como which they said was like stepping back to the 1920's only with Internet access…

"Do you think we'll see George Clooney in the bar again?" another quip from Lynn.

They would have short stops in Prague, Barcelona, London to visit friends and then ten days in Paris, their favorite place. With Paris being the headquarters of the travel company, they had lots of friends there. Russ said he just wanted to walk the streets and eat 'pain au chocolate' (chocolate croissants to Americans)."

They were going to end their trip with a week in New York. They had tickets to a couple of shows Lynn wanted to see, and Russ had old business partners there.

It was a nine week trip in total, but they both still lamented about how many great places they were skipping. But they wanted to get back in time to hold their big annual July Fourth party at the Farm.

Diana told me that Russ and Lynn had been throwing their July Fourth event for about ten years, and it had grown to about 250 guests for this coming year. It was a simple affair, basically pizza, chicken and ice cream. But between the game room, magicians and fortune tellers, and the other entertainment they hired, it was always great fun. Because of the fire hazard, fireworks were replaced with a laser light show that amazed even the techies in attendance.

The rest of the dinner that evening was consumed with all the fun details of the trip and the July Fourth party.

As our new 'tradition' would have it, Russ and I got berries and ice cream while the kids went to the game room. Lynn and Diana came over to join us. We had started to talk more about Paris when Russ visibly winched and put his bowl down.

Another attack?

"You okay?" I asked.

"Yes," he said, "But I am having an attack... I'm going to head to my room."

Lynn gave him her arm, and he walked slowly to his bedroom.

Diana looked at me scared. I tried to comfort her. "I saw one of these attacks two weeks ago. He seemed to do just fine with it."

"I know," she said, "but it still scares me."

Scares the shit out of me too, but I don't want to show it or Diana might really flip out...

"Hopefully it's only another short attack for him."

Just then there was a loud sound from Russ in his room. It sounded like 'Ow'.

Lynn came running in. "I think we need to go to the hospital for this one. I discussed it with Russ a couple of months ago. He said drive him to Stanford. It will be quicker and better than 911 as there is nothing they can do for him in an ambulance. He has taken oxycodone. Hopefully that will help."

Diana spoke before I could, "I will get the SUV. Jay, I think Anna went to her cottage. Can you tell her what happened and ask her to come back to the house for the kids until we return?"

By the time I got back with Anna, Lynn and Diana had helped Russ out the front door. I ran up the steps to join them.

Getting him up these stairs must have been painful...

I got there in time to help get Russ into the passenger seat.

"No belt," he said. "It hurts too much to have pressure on it."

Diana had already gotten into the driver's seat. Lynn and I climbed in the back. I sat behind Russ.

I do not remember much of the trip to the hospital. Diana tried to drive the curvy roads as fast as she could without having the beltless Russ jostled too much. I tried to hold his shoulders steady from behind to help. Shortly after we started, the seat belt alarm went off and the only way I could figure out how to turn it off was buckle the belt behind the seat.

Russ had put a small towel in his mouth to bite on when the waves of pain got too much for him. The oxycodone helped, but you could see by Russ's face that the pain just raced by it. There were a couple of minutes where Russ seemed to lose consciousness from the pain. I felt the pulse in his neck and calmed a near panicked Lynn, who momentarily thought we might have lost him.

Diana drove to the emergency entrance. Lynn and I put Russ between us and half carried him directly to the entrance. There was a metal detector to go through, but at this hour it was not manned. We did not wait, but walked right through.

The metal detector alarm went off. A security guard who had been standing by the admittance desk immediately headed our way, telling us we would have to go through the metal detector again. But when he saw the look on Russ's face, he changed his mind and instead helped us get Russ to the admissions window. There were a few other people sitting in the waiting area, but the guard said he would take Russ right in if Lynn would give all the necessary information to admissions.

Since Russ was already in the Stanford Hospital computer system, all his admission information was there, including his listing Lynn as spouse. This listing gave her total access to everything…

I wondered, *are they secretly married?*

Before we finished the registration, Diana came in from parking the car. The guard did stop her and made her give him her purse and car keys before she went through the metal detector. She kind of looked at it funny, but apparently emergency patients and their companions had come here with handguns and knives before. This could be a problem later.

I found out later that the front entry to the hospital had no metal detector. It was only the emergency room. That was some kind of statement on the emotional state of people who are in the middle of emergencies…

After registration, we were shown to Russ's bed. Lynn had 'announced' us as Russ's children just in case there was any problem.

Hmmm… maybe they are not married, and it is just to get through hospital rules, like Diana and me being children…

When I saw Russ, he already had an IV in his arm and was still wide awake.

"We did a quick blood test for a pancreatitis attack and it was positive," the doctor said. "So we have given him morphine. It seems to be helping. But the amylase count is so high, we may have to give him some fentanyl for pain."

Russ was awake enough to talk a bit. "Ah… I see my A team is here." Then turning to the doctor he said, "Everything is fine now, Doc."

Then he winched in pain to show that was not really the case.

A few minutes later, the doctor administered the fentanyl. On my IPhone, I looked the drug up on the Internet. It said it was 80 to 100 times more powerful than morphine.

Shit… this is serious stuff…

I decided not to say anything to Lynn and Diana. They were both talking to Russ and trying to distract him from his pain. Russ seemed to relax a bit and then a bit more. Finally, he was asleep.

Mostly, I kept my eyes glued to the monitoring screen trying to decipher any movement in his condition. I had asked one doctor what some of the numbers on the screen meant and what they were most concerned about. His vital signs seemed okay, however.

The hospital staff kept Russ semi-asleep for the next three hours. And after they felt they had stabilized him, they admitted him to the hospital proper, and he was moved to a regular room.

The three of us sat in his room not saying much. At some point, the night nurse told us that he was going to be sleeping for quite a while and that maybe we would want to get some sleep ourselves. Lynn said she wanted to stay. The nurses set up a small cot for her, and Diana and I left. We said we would be back in the morning and also told Lynn to call if anything happened.

Diana said she wanted to drive as she knew the route better than me. Diana and I talked a bit on the drive back to the Farm. We were both worried about Russ.

A couple of weeks ago after Russ had told me about his pancreatitis, I had searched the Internet to read more about the illness including what would happen after a serious acute pancreas attack. I told Diana the basic information which was that Russ would probably be in the hospital for a week. Most of that time, he would be feed through his IV, so that his pancreas could recover. Eventually, they would give him a liquid diet and finally a bit of solid food. If he could handle that without any recurrence of problems, he could go home.

In reality, there was no 'fixing' the pancreas. The only thing to do was to give the patient pain killers, stop eating and wait for the pancreas to heal itself as best as it could. Researchers were trying to make transplants work, but no success at this point.

It was after three in morning when we got home. We had kept Anna informed by phone from the emergency room. Finally, we were able to tell her that Russ was going to be all right. She had gone to sleep in one of the guest rooms to be in the house when the kids woke in the morning.

Diana wrote a note for Anna in the kitchen telling her that we got home late and would probably get up late.

When I finally got to my cottage, I was exhausted from the roller coaster day. But I did not fall asleep right away. My mind was still full of thoughts. It shook me to see Russ looking so pale and hooked up to all the wires and tubes monitoring him…

Will he really be Okay?... What does Okay mean if you have a fatal illness?...

The more I thought about it all, the worse it got.

It is such a gift for me to be with him... He is only sixty-eight. Why would God take him now?... He is just teaching his grandkids how to really enjoy their lives...

It may have been thirty minutes or maybe an hour, but I did finally fall asleep.

25

The days Russ was in the hospital all seem to run together in my mind.

Russ was groggy on Saturday and really woke up on Sunday afternoon. By Monday he had substantially reduced his pain medication and was starting to walk the halls with his IV pole attached to him. I visited every day, sometimes with Diana or Lynn and sometimes alone. Alex, Alicia and Kevin came after school on Monday.

After the hi's and hugs, Alicia asked, "GP, what happens next?"

"You mean to me or to you?" he teased her.

"To you. Silly. I am not the one lying in a hospital bed."

"To me? I'm coming home as soon as I can. Anna makes better food than they give me here and I can see no other reason to stay."

"How soon is soon?"

I love the way she always asks the tough questions…

"As soon as my pancreas is healed enough," he answered. "They test that by giving me Jell-O, and if I can eat it without getting sick, I can go home. It could be tomorrow or Wednesday.

"OK… I was thinking of making you a welcome home cake, and I wanted know when I needed to do it."

Russ smiled. "So, you're going for my favorite grandchild award? You just might win with a cake."

Alex burst in, "I could let you beat me in air hockey a couple of times."

"Ah… competition. I love it." Then he turned to Kevin. "You want to get in on this?"

"Not right now. Maybe later."

Russ laughed. "Good answer. No reason to reveal your plans to your competitors."

I loved watching Russ in action with his ability to use humor to lighten any situation. I had watched him tease his nurses, doctors, even other patients he saw while walking in the hall (he offered to race one guy in a wheelchair… when he lost, he said to the guy, 'Same time tomorrow?')

Russ had told me that he thought humor was one of his keys to happiness. 'If you can make someone else smile, it will make you feel happier'. I liked the simple way he phrased it.

Russ came home on Thursday. Alicia made a cake, Alex promised to lose at air hockey and Kevin... he surprised everyone with a song he had created just for Russ. It was the first song he ever named. He called it 'My GP'.

When Kevin played his song, I thought Russ was going to cry. The words that Kevin had added to the song were very touching. It had phrases like, 'when I am sad, I just think of GP and a smile comes to my face', and 'when I grow up, I just want one thing, to be like GP.'

Within a day or two, life had pretty much returned to normal, except Russ was now limited to a liquid diet. So his meals consisted of two cans of Ensure. Chocolate was his favorite. Sometimes Anna would add some ice cream and make a 'milk shake' out of it. Russ's comment was, "Delicious Anna. McDonald's could make a fortune if they added this recipe to their menu. They could capture the 'seniors' market."

One question in my mind while Russ was recovering in the hospital was whether he and Lynn were still taking their big trip. They were scheduled to fly to Tokyo in just a week. I knew they wanted to, but with all the possible complications I wasn't sure if they really could.

So that first night Russ was home at dinner he offered a toast (with Ensure – in a wine glass). "Lynn and I wanted to toast the six of you. I know we have had a lot of fun the last three months, but Lynn and I made the decision last night that we 'need' to take our trip."

I remember thinking. *I love it… he is living every day as best he can… why say 'no' when you can say 'yes'…*

Everyone else at dinner seemed more surprised than I was… everyone except Lynn, of course. But, there were no 'naysayers'. No one said 'it's too hard, too unsafe, or don't go'.

When it came to the Word game, it was Kevin's turn. He passed saying his song was his word, so Russ said.

"Alicia, it's your turn then." She held up her hand palm out in the 'stop' sign and thought for a few seconds.

"Okay, I have it. This is for both of you. What are you looking forward to most on this trip and why?"

Russ laughed. "No pressure, Alicia. Lynn, do you want to go first?"

"No Russ, go ahead." She was stalling a bit was my guess.

"Well, Alicia, I think for me it might be seeing your Mom and Dad in Mongolia. I have never been to Mongolia, so it will be a new experience for me. And your Mom and Dad are taking us out into the wilderness to some of the villages where they are doing their research. It should be a very interesting experience."

He continued, "That said, I must add that I'm really excited to do everything. One reason to go now is that we planned this trip so well that I don't want to miss any of it."

Russ looked at Lynn, "Ready?"

"Of course…" she answered. "In a word Alicia, Paris… I love walking around just stopping in stores, buying snacks and trinkets, or just looking at the neat way they decorate their store windows. It was on a trip to Paris that I fell in love with your grandfather, and it still has a special place in my heart.

Mongolia or Paris… sure wouldn't be hard for me to pick…

As if reading my mind, Russ looked at Alicia and said, "And if you were coming on the trip, which place would you pick?"

Again, Alicia thought for a few seconds, "Positano. I looked at some pictures on the Internet and it looked very cool built on a hillside with a beach." She looked over at Lynn and added, "And pizza at Chez Black sounds good too."

"Nice, I love those things too," Russ said. "And Alex, do you have a favorite."

Alex knew he would get called on, so he was ready. "I heard Prague is very cool. So it might be fun to see it."

A party town for Alex, check…" Russ smiled at
And Kevin?"

"Paris," he said without hesitation.

"Paris… hmmm… why Paris, Kevin?"

"They have Euro Disney there."

It was stated like the fact it was. No further explanation needed.

Anna, Diana, and I all had favorites – two Paris, one Lake Como. I was the Lake Como. I had heard from friends that Lake Como was stunning.

After dinner, Russ and I had our berries and ice cream again – although for Russ, Anne put his berries through the blender and liquefied them. I asked him how he had made his decision to go on the trip.

"Sometimes when I have a decision to make and there just doesn't seem to be a right or wrong choice, I use my book method."

Did he say book method???

"My book method is where I pretend that my life is a book I am reading and I'm the main character in this book. Then, I ask myself, if I was reading this book which choice would I want the main character to take… in this case it would be either 'stay home or go'?"

"I decided as the reader of 'my book', I would want him to go on the trip because I would want to read about what happened on that trip... so decision made. We're going..."

He continued, "I have used the book method many times, and for the most part I've been happy with the decisions it gave me."

I marveled one more time at yet another lesson in happiness creation. If you viewed your life like a good book, your life would probably be a 'good book'.

I need to remember to write this one down...

"Another interesting idea," I said weakly. Actually, it was better than just another idea. So I added, "It's an idea I will try to use myself. How do you remember to use it?"

"Good question. I'm not sure. At this point, I just sort of use it quite a bit, and it's natural for me to sometimes think of my life as a book."

Just then, Lynn and Diana joined us, and we talked more trip plans.

Kevin, Alicia and Alex all came back in pajamas ready for their GP bedtime story. This time they told GP they wanted adventure travel as the story theme...

26

Time flew quickly. Saturday, I helped get some things together for their trip. The oddest chore was shipping cases of Ensure to their hotels in Mongolia, China, and India. Since Russ had to be on his liquid diet for at least 30 days, he was going to need a good supply. And just in case they could not find a good substitute in these countries, he wanted to be prepared. We put two six packs in the luggage as well.

On Sunday afternoon, there was a big family barbeque at the Farm. Except for Katlin and her husband, who were in Mongolia, everyone else was in attendance. It was a nice group, eight kids and eight adults.

Anna had put on another feast, barbequing fish and chicken at the same time. She added her usual addition of salads and vegetables. It was fantastic.

It was Goth twin Charlotte's turn for the Word game. She had been pretty reserved so far, so I wondered what she would ask. I looked at Russ to see if he was concerned. The opposite... he seemed eager to hear her question.

"Family. Why is family important?" she asked.

I wasn't expecting that one. I wondered if Charlotte was hoping Russ would fail or for some reason, she was really trying to figure out why she should care.

"Good timing for that question." Russ was referring to the fact that almost all of his family was sitting around the table.

"I would start with two things I think are important in understanding family. First is that for different people and different families, the importance of family varies from zero to being the most important facet in a life. Second would be that there are lots of different 'families' that people can have. There is the one you are born into or are raised by. Another is the one you might marry into, and another is the one you create with children. And another one is the 'family' you can create with your friends."

"Charlotte," Russ looked at her. "I assume you were intending to focus mainly on the family you grow up with, correct?"

"Ah…. yeah."

Russ continued, "Okay, let's start there…"

"One thing most family members have is time… time with you. You're sixteen now. Your mom and dad and sister have been in your life for most of the sixteen years you have been alive. Not every day of your life, but most of them. This means you have a lot of common experiences; schools, vacations, pets, friends, etc. You have your aunts, uncles, and cousins in common, and you even have Lynn, Anna, Diana, Jay and me… and the Farm in common."

"It turns out that this much common experience will be a rare thing for most people the rest of their lives. For most people only 'family' will have this much of a common bond."

"Let's add to that 'common bond', the love that some family members give each other. If you ever watch parents of babies and little children, you can see the love and support they give. What you may not see is how often the child is giving unconditional love in return. Sometimes they will 'hang on' every word a parent or older sibling says."

"For me that is what allows 'family' to be important, but it can be destroyed as well. Taken for granted, the love and support from your family may eventually be crushed. Not quickly, but eventually."

"The media makes a big deal out of married people getting divorces, but it's just as common for family members to 'divorce' each other. Like the sisters who grow to hate each other, and when they become adults, they never see or talk to each other. When that happens, all that common bond and history of support is withdrawn and lost."

"Most people do better when they have this l₍ support, so they will need to replace it with love and support from elsewhere. Or they escape to alcohol or drugs to hide from their own reality."

"That is my answer to your question – did it help?"

Charlotte had no instant response.

I wonder if the 'drugs' reference has her thinking… hopefully.

Her Mom, Monique, then spoke up, "So you're saying family is very important?"

Russ responded, "Ah… what I was trying to say was that family 'can' be very important. At least some kind of family, as it can be the love and support a person needs to do well and feel good about themselves. "

He continued, "But I also feel you have to 'let go' in a family. Family members should not be required to treat each other as important just because they're related. When you set someone free, then you will have to earn the importance in their lives by what you do, not just your genetic connection. This is why for some people I think that their best 'family' is not the genetic one, but the one they put together with friends or at work. These are the people who have 'earned' their way to being treated like 'family.'"

I watched the kids when Russ said 'let go'. Charlotte smiled a bit, and Dan and Loren both nodded a bit. I was not surprised, and I wondered with that comment if Russ was actually trying to speak more to Brenda than to Monique or Charlotte.

Everyone was quiet for a second. Then Kevin spoke.

"Are their more drumsticks?"

Sometimes the most important thing in the world is not high level thoughts, but just a hungry stomach...

Anna answered. "Yes, on the counter. There were quite a few left when I took mine."

With that break in the conversation, once again the trip became the main topic.

The table only broke up when Anna mentioned her desserts, pumpkin pie, Russ's all-time favorite, and homemade strawberry shortcake, Lynn's favorite. There was enough whip cream and ice cream that even if you didn't like the basic dessert you could fill your plate with those and nuts, cherries, and hot fudge. For Russ she had she had a bowl of just pie filling and whip cream.

Very quickly, the kids finished and hit the game room, leaving just the adults at the table. I hadn't noticed it before, but Mark had a number of Russ's mannerisms and his speech pattern and calmness. He seemed to be an easy-going, happy person. I was glad, as Brenda's controlling nature could be hard on the kids, and this counterbalance was good.

Monique on the other hand did not seem at ease. I wondered if she still was suffering from her divorce and somehow feeling like she had failed her Dad.

Russ had said there is more here than I can see… I wonder if Diana knows… maybe later I can ask her…

The evening did not go too late. It was a school night, and both Mark, Monique (and their families) had drives of almost an hour to get home.

27

Before I knew it, Wednesday morning had arrived and I was helping load bags into the SUV. Diana was the designated driver to go to the airport.

Alex, Alicia, and Kevin said goodbye at breakfast before Anna took them to school. Not seeing GP and Lynn for two months was a big deal for them and the goodbyes included heavy hugs and some tears from Alicia when she waved at GP from the car.

The good news was that the same week that Russ and Lynn were returning, their parents would be returning as well. It was going to be a big reunion week for the kids.

About an hour after the kids left, the SUV was loaded and Diana got in the driver's seat. Lynn gave me a hug and said.

"Have fun with the kids these next two months."

"I'm sure I will. They're lots of fun."

Russ came over and also gave me a hug.

Russ never hugs…

I assumed the hug was because of the long time they would be gone.

"Remember to believe in yourself and treat

like a great book. Happiness will surely follow," h

"Got it," I had mastered that…

Not Pursued

He hopped in, and they were gone.

I went back into the house, and it felt very empty. Amazing how a presence like Russ's could be so strong that just one minute after he left I was already missing him.

The next seven weeks went by as quickly as the previous three months I had spent on the Farm.

The kids were busy with school events especially end-of-the-year school events. I made it to five school music programs in two weeks.

We altered the Word game a bit, so that Anna, Diana and I took turns trying to answer topics. Alex helped with constant Internet searches. Even I got familiar with Wikipedia (which in 2008 was still somewhat new).

I bought a big map of the world and put it on an easel near the kitchen table. We tracked where in the world Russ and Lynn were on the map.

Russ and Lynn called once from each city, and starting in Tokyo, they bought something 'of interest' for each of the kids in each city. They shipped the items back, and when the box arrived (about a week after shipping) we would wait for their next call and then open it. That way

Russ and Lynn could tell the kids why they bought what they did while the kids were opening the boxes.

Lynn had a Facebook page, and she posted photos on it frequently. My favorite was Russ with the Terracotta Soldiers in Xian. They are full-sized sculptures, and somehow Russ got down on the exhibit floor. Standing next to a group of stone soldiers was a pretty cool photo.

All this was a great way to get the kids really into the trip.

I had gone into Fenwick & West the day after Russ and Lynn left. I picked a project I wanted to help on. It was a bit of a research project on international intellectual property protection laws. It was a project for one of their mid-sized clients who was just starting to expand operations internationally.

I worked on my legal project during the day, while Diana worked with Russ's five operating companies. Russ had done a good job of getting Diana into a position of being of value to his partners. So during the Russ and Lynn calls, Diana would ask Russ a couple of business questions. Russ would then say 'I'm working hard to help pay for the trip...'

At night, we played with the kids and often worked with Anna on the big July Fourth party that would occur a week after Russ and Lynn returned. It was fun for me as I had never done anything to help plan an event this size.

After seven weeks, Lynn and Russ were just getting to Paris, Lynn's favorite city. Diana and I spoke to Pierre before they arrived there, and he had a few extra events planned for them during the week.

They called on their third night in Paris. They were giddy with laughter. They had just gone shopping for the kids at the Paris Flea Market and were obviously pleased with their selections. All had been shipped they said.

Kevin asked what they liked the most so far in Paris.

Russ answered, "You won't think this is cool Kevin, but one day you will. Our best event so far was walking from our apartment on rue Montorgueil to Saint Germain across the river last night after dinner. It was a warm night. We had some chocolate crepes in a café we like over there. We watched all the Parisian couples walking by just enjoying the nice warm evening."

"I think I would prefer Euro Disney"

Russ laughed. "Probably, Kevin, probably"

Alicia said, "Sounds good for you two, and the part about the crepes sounds good to me."

After a few more minutes, the call was over.

28

It was Saturday, and for the kids, everyday now felt like Saturday. Summer vacation from school had started a week ago, and the kids were in full vacation mode already.

Alex was starting tennis camp on Monday. Alicia and a friend were going to Los Angeles with Diana next week for a three-day visit. And Kevin was already in computer camp at Stanford. The computer camp was for older kids, but Kevin's teacher knew someone at the camp and had told them Kevin could handle it.

Their parents would be arriving that next Sunday, and Russ and Lynn were scheduled to be back on the Thursday following.

With all the kid activities, Anna, Diana and I were busier now than during the school year.

But today was a 'goof off' day.

Alex and I went surfing early in the morning. Alicia and I were doing a short afternoon ride. It was only our fourth ride since Bronco had died. and Alicia was just riding whatever horse Harry saddled up for her. When I got back,

Kevin was going to let me hear one of his new songs that was not finished yet.

After working out the details on how Kevin needed to 'protect' his songs and collect the appropriate royalties when they got played, I sent a second song to the radio station. It was already a top twenty request in just its first week. So 'This Kid' now had two songs in the top forty at the same time.

After the busy day, Diana and I played games with the kids until late. I had found out I was better at bowling than Alex so to make up for my constantly losing at air hockey, I 'made' him bowl with me occasionally, and tonight was one of those nights.

When I went to bed, I wrote more in my journal. I had continued to do this, making notes about each day. After that, I read a bit of Dick Francis, I was now on my fifth book of his, obviously I enjoyed them.

I must have fallen asleep reading. I woke up to loud banging on my door. It was dark outside, but my light was still on, and the Kindle fell on the floor as I jumped out of bed.

When I finally focused, I could hear it was Diana yelling my name as she pounded on the door. Somehow I had gotten into the habit of locking the cottage door when I slept.

I know there was zero chance of a stranger coming in, but for some reason I sleep better knowing it was locked.

I opened the door and Diana came in.

"Russ has had another attack."

Shit, that's not good...

"They took him to the hospital, but he didn't make it. Jay, Russ is dead."

What??? Not now, not before I could see him again... Shit...

Diana just hugged me and cried. I didn't say anything. I just hugged her back.

We both knew this would happen sometime, but I guess neither of us thought it would be this soon.

Oh Russ... why you?... why not give you more time???

My mind was suffering the loss.

Finally I asked, "How did you hear?"

"I got a call on my phone from Pierre. He said he was having lunch with Lynn and Russ when the attack happened. He called an ambulance, and they got Russ to the hospital, but he died there after only an hour. Apparently, there was nothing they could do to save him."

All I could say was, "I know… Russ had told me that it could end this way. And I guess after the first big attack, I should've thought more about this possibility… but I didn't."

"Me neither."

Then she let go of me and spoke, "I told Pierre I would get to Paris as fast as I can. He said he can help Lynn, but I told him I was coming anyway."

Always prepared with a plan, no matter what… she is one strong woman.

She continued, "I'm going to call Mark now. I'm pretty sure he will want to go to Paris with me. I think someone from the family will probably need to be there."

She started to cry again, and I felt tears come to my own eyes.

She said, "He was so special, so special to me. No one has ever taught me more about life than he did. It's just so sad…"

"I know," I whispered. I was working hard not to cry. I'm not sure why I was working so hard, I guess it's that male thing to be strong to help a female. Anyway I held it together, and she called Mark.

She was able to reach him. Mark was not as surprised as I thought he would be. Apparently Russ had told him after the first big attack that it could happen suddenly and at any time.

Diana was right. Mark wanted to join her on the next flight out. She said she would book the flights as soon as possible and let him know.

I got dressed and walked up to the house with Diana. She had left her computer in her office and needed it to find the quickest flight.

We decided to let Anna and the kids sleep and stayed in the office area of the house. We talked through how Anna and I could handle the kids and that we would make whatever plans were necessary once she got to Paris, which would be Monday morning at the earliest.

I told her I would call Monique and track down Katlin and also let Fenwick & West know and find out what if anything we needed to do.

It turned out Diana could get tickets on an 11 AM non-stop flight to Paris, and she called Mark to tell him. With that she went down to her cottage to pack, while I stayed to track down Katlin.

I was able to reach her. She and her husband were in Hong Kong now. Like Mark, Katlin did not seem totally surprised. Again, when Russ was in Mongolia, he had told her it could be sudden. She told me she wished she could have seen him again back in California, but she knew that her father would think that having a few great days in Paris would be good end to a wonderful life.

I was struck with how peaceful Katlin was. I guess when you knew how Russ felt about everything, you knew he was at peace with it all. That meant you were sad, but not overwhelmed with grief.

I was not at that level of acceptance. I was still shaken by Russ's death.

I decided to wait until 8 AM before calling Monique and that time gave me some time alone to think.

Russ would tell me to be happy. Not let something that has happened ruin my today or my tomorrow… then it occurred to me that I should be happy that I decided to come to California to work with him. I almost didn't come, and so I almost missed out on a chance of a lifetime to learn about life from him. And while my time with Russ was short, I had learned more about being happy in three months than I had in twenty-seven years. In reality, Russ was a gift that I should be happy I got…

Eventually, I heard Anna down in the kitchen. I went down to tell her. She said Diana had told her down at her cottage. We talked for a few minutes about the kids and the news. Anna felt they would be sad, but not inconsolable. She said maybe we could tell them together. I agreed.

Anna also seemed to be at ease with Russ dying. I was starting to understand that you really can look at an event as sad as this one and deal with it as part of life, not a crisis.

Monique was different. She exploded with grief on the phone. I consoled her best as I could, but after Mark, Katlin, and Anna's acceptance, I was now a bit surprised that Monique reacted so strongly. Then I realized she was reacting more normally. She did not have the internal happiness that the others had. At that moment, I wondered why, but I let that thought go. I needed to focus on calming her.

I gave Monique an outline of the plan. Mark and Diana were going today to Paris to help Lynn, and more details would follow after they got there.

When I hung up, she was no longer hysterical, but I thought she might start up again for any reason.

It ended up that I told the three kids what had happened while Anna and Diana were standing with me at the breakfast table. Somehow it seemed natural that I should tell them. I think it was because I had become 'one of them'.

And being in this position, it was easier for me to deliver bad news.

They all looked sad. Even Kevin understood the finality of Russ's death. I proposed that they ride with me to the airport when I took Diana and then we might go up to San Francisco afterwards and walk along the shore at Crissy Fields.

I really felt leaving them right now was not the best idea.

We dropped Diana off at the airport. Then, we went up to San Francisco to the Presidio and parked at Crissy Fields. It had turned sunny, and the view across the bay from the Golden Gate Bridge all the way to Berkeley was stunning. Quite a few sailboats were out racing around in the glorious weather.

While we walked, we took turns talking about the things we had learned from GP. It proved to be very helpful.

However, just when I thought they were feeling a bit stronger, Alex looked up at me and spoke. "This means I will never get to play air hockey with GP again." Tears started to just steam down his face. Kevin was now crying and saying he would never hear another GP bedtime story. Alicia just stood still and looked sad.

What are the things you would wish you would never being able to do again?

I found a stone wall, and we all sat on it looking out at the bay. Such a beautiful sight on such a sad day… There was little I could think to say except, "I know... I know' which I kept repeating to them.

That night we watched movies after dinner, and we all went to bed a bit early. I thought about trying a story, but I wisely pulled back from that idea. Not only was I no match for GP, but it was not what they needed. They needed time to heal.

29

Once Mark and Diana were in Paris for a day, the plans solidified. Russ had asked to be cremated, so that would be done in France, and everyone would be back in San Francisco by July 1st. It was further decided to go ahead with the July Fourth event and make it a celebration of Russ's life and not a memorial.

Once they announced the go-ahead plans for July Fourth, the number of committed attendees doubled the expected attendance. Confirmed attendance was now more than 500 people, all wanting to honor Russ. Many people were flying in, including many of his current and ex-partners and their families. Pierre, Bertrand and Thomas were also flying in from Paris.

This increase in attendance put a strain on Anna and me. Anna was in charge of the food, and now she needed to recalculate. I was busy trying to redo the logistics that Diana had arranged. I needed to add enough tables, chairs, serving places, plates and even figure out where and how the extra parking would work out in the best way.

The most unusual thing that happened to me was a call from Matt Lawson at Fenwick & West. He called say that if the will Russ signed just before he left on the trip was his last one, then I was Russ's appointed executor. He said they would have a meeting to go over the will with the family once everyone was back, but he wanted me to know the situation and that it would be good if I attended that family meeting.

I immediately wondered why Russ had decided to give me that job instead of one of his kids or Matt Lawson himself. So I asked Matt. He explained that Russ thought the combination of my obvious love for the grandkids, appreciation of the Farm, recent knowledge of all the business matters, and being a lawyer made me perfect for the job.

Katlin and her husband landed at SFO on Sunday, and I picked them up. After spending four months with their kids, I knew a lot about them. And they were just as I expected. Katlin was an adult Alicia, full of questions and pretty much a driver. Her husband was more like a combination of Alex and Kevin, thoughtful but with an adventurous side.

I brought them back to the Farm as they had taken on a short rental of their house in Portola Valley which they had extended through the end of June. They had decided to move into one of the cottages for a couple of weeks until they could put their personal belongings back in their house. It also worked best not to move the kids right now.

July 1st came quickly and with it the return of Lynn, Diana, and Mark. The whole family had decided to move onto the Farm upon their return with Monique and the twins and Mark's family also moving in on the 2nd.

My mother came out on July 2nd as well. She stayed in my cottage. I moved to sleep on the sofa in the living area for a few days. She was very helpful as usual, and it was good to see her connect with all the people I had told her about in our phone calls over the last four months.

There was also one mystery she was finally willing to clear up for me. When Russ told me he was dying, he answered the mystery of 'Why now?' But the question of 'Why me?' had never come up

So on the second night my mother was in my cottage, I decided to ask her again. This time she told me that 'Uncle Russ' had often called her to see how I was doing after my father had died. She asked him questions, and he gave her advice as he always did. When he called in February, she told him of my depressed state. That is when Russ came up with his 'adventure' for me and asked my mother what she thought of it. She said 'yes' it was a great idea. And as a result my whole life had forever changed.

It was probably good that the whole family was at the Farm, as there was a great deal of work to do to prepare for the July 4th event. So many out-of-town guests coming in added to the usual complexity. Luckily, at least one of Russ's children, Mark, Monique or Katlin, knew most of the guests and would be 'assigned' to greet them (even if just on the phone) and make sure they knew where the Farm was and when to come. Of course, some of them came out to the Farm the day before to see if they could 'help', which, as expected, just slowed things down.

In the end, it all worked out well. With Russ's usual luck, July Fourth proved to be a gorgeous sunny day at the Farm. The event was scheduled from 4 PM to 10 PM, but people started showing up at noon.

The grandkids took over the job of finding parking for everyone. Basically they just kept moving people down the road past the cottages and parking where there was space without blocking the road. Then four of the grandkids operated the golf carts to bring the guests back up to the main house.

The house was set up to entertain as Russ always would. There was non-stop food. Some of the horses were brought up for kids to ride. A small stage was set up for a couple of magicians to perform. The biggest hit was the fortune tellers. The three of them were set up in the offices, and the line was never shorter than ten deep to see them.

Despite the celebration atmosphere, and our no-memorial effort, it didn't exactly work out that way. Don't get me wrong. Everyone was having the fun time Russ would have wanted. It was just that a few people really wanted to address everyone and say some words about Russ.

There turned out to be six people who really wanted to speak. And despite a great effort to keep each person to less than five minutes, it was still over a half hour of listening.

There was a sound system set up that Russ had used in the past to greet everyone (Mark and Lynn did the greeting this year).

The speakers were four men and two women, and each gave a warm remembrance of Russ. Only two cried as they spoke. It was touching, so touching that the large crowd stayed very quiet as each spoke. The shortest and my favorite was the very last speaker. I think Russ would have loved it.

"Hello. My name is Peter Lincoln and I met Russ in grade school when we were both eight years old. So I guess it has been sixty years of friendship."

"Russ was always smart and had a wonderful sense of humor, but over the years I think he found what I term his 'calling'. His 'calling' was that of a person who was able to bring happiness to his life and the lives of everyone around him."

"Over the years he got so good at this, that I think everyone who knew him felt that if they were feeling low they just needed to talk to Russ for five minutes, and he would have them laughing again. He did this all the time."

"I think we can all agree that Russ knew how to live life…"

"I can testify that in his life, Russ gave much more than he took… and he took a lot."

Then he handed the microphone back to Mark.

When I heard those words I thought…

I hope someday someone can say that about me….

+ + + + + + +

+ + + + + + +

30

It has been six years since my first visit to the Farm and when people first read this story, they often asked, 'What happened after that? What happened to everyone?'

So I added this little section to bring you up to 2014.

Mark and his family still live in Los Gatos, California, and when I see Mark, I notice that each year he looks a bit more like Russ. He left Google for a start-up about two years after Russ died and is still there. He seems to be doing very well, and he is the same happy person he was in 2008.

His wife, Brenda, wasn't able to change her controlling nature, but she was able to channel it away from her kids a bit. She started raising seeing-eye dogs, a good place for her energy. I think she is on her third one now.

Marci is now 18 and a senior in high school. She added film making to her love of music and has been accepted to USC in Los Angeles where she will start in the fall with the future plan of attending their film school. Over the past six years, she has got closer to Alicia and Kevin and has been a frequent visitor to the Farm.

Loren just finished her junior year at UCSB (the university of California at Santa Barbara) where she is majoring in math and partying. Both of these 'activities' are well established there.

Dan graduated from Vanderbilt University with a Computer Science degree two years ago. He hurt his ankle in his sophomore year and had to give up competitive tennis. That may not have been so bad, as he then focused fully on computer science. He moved to San Francisco after college. During the day, he works for Twitter, but nights and weekends, he and two buddies are trying to build their first start-up. As to girls, I see a new one every three months. I suppose they don't like competing with the start-up.

Monique has struggled quite a bit. I'm not sure how much emotional support she got from Russ over the years, but after he died she went downhill quickly. Her alcohol abuse became a problem. Mark, Katlin, and Lynn stepped in as much as they could, and Monique finally checked into an alcohol rehab center. After a couple of relapses, she has been sober for over two years now and is rebuilding her life. She lost the art gallery during this period, but she took a job teaching art at one of the art academies and seems to like it. More importantly she has had a serious boyfriend the last six months, and that experience has added to her personal self-confidence.

Her daughter, Estelle, moved to New York after high school to try modeling. She got a few jobs, but ended up being a waitress to pay the rent. After a year of this, she decided to go to college in New York. That lasted a year, as she really had no motivation and flunked out. She moved to Los Angeles to live with a much older man she had met in New York. This lasted a year as well, and then she moved to Maui and got a job as a bartender in a really good sushi restaurant. She became interested in being a sushi chef, and the lead chef took an interest in her and started to give her lessons. Over the next year she learned enough to start preparing sushi under his direction. The last time I saw her was the happiest that I have ever seen her.

Charlotte started to have more serious problems within six months of Russ's death. Drugs were becoming a focal point of her life. She ran away from home that October. After about a month, she came back. She looked like a different girl. When she was 17, she ran away again. This time she cut all contact except on her 18th birthday she called her mother and told her not to look for her. At 22, she is still out of control with no signs of wanting to change, but at least she calls her mother a couple times a year.

Katlin and her husband are both still professors at Stanford, and they still live in Portola Valley. They took their research project in 2008 and turned it into their first book which was highly regarded. The Obama administration asked Katlin to work on a commission on women's economics worldwide and how it can influence peace. This last year they were mentioned by some people as possible Nobel Prize nominees for their ground-breaking analysis of village financial systems and how to impact them positively.

Besides beating me at air hockey every chance he gets, Alex has also managed to grow up. He will be a junior at the University of Wisconsin this fall majoring in electrical engineering. But like Loren, he seems to have a double major in party attendance and fraternity life, perfect for a 20-year old. His Facebook page is not X-rated... yet. He had an internship last summer at Twitter, thanks to his cousin, Dan. This summer, he is headed to WhatsApp. He told me he's also doing 'weekend projects' for Dan's start-up venture. I half wonder if he will make it through his last two years with all these distractions.

Alicia is finishing her senior year at high school. She has taken that twelve-year old going on twenty-two personality and turned it into a force to be reckoned with. She is Class President and Captain of the school soccer team.

With help from her parents and her cousin, Dan, when she was 16 she started a small online fashion jeans line. Through an online designer chat room, she 'met' a designer in Australia. With the help of her parents' friends in Hong Kong, she got the designs made in China. With Dan's help, she built a web store. Using social media, she started to make sales. Six months ago, she got a break when a reality TV show actress mentioned her label on a talk show. Last month, her parents helped her hire a part-time person to handle all the logistics. She tells me she still has no time for boys yet, except she has time to work with her younger brother Kevin.

Probably the most unusual six years have been Kevin's. He has stayed a math genius, and although he is only a 15-year old high school freshman, he spends 8 am to 11 am every morning taking classes at Stanford University. From noon to 3 pm, he is back at the high school.

But the real story is his music. As 'This Kid', Kevin has produced over a dozen hit songs. Dim Mak Records started producing his songs last year, and Atlantic Records just signed a distribution deal. He is in high demand at clubs in the San Francisco Bay Area (and he has made one trip to Berlin, London, and New York). His manager is the great negotiator and sister, Alicia -- with some legal help of course. At clubs, his cousin, Dan, is his chaperone. Dan seems to be the cousin who helps all the cousins. This music success has given Kevin a level of social status in high school that is almost celebrity. It is counterbalanced by his previous total lack of social skills, as he is still a true geek by nature. The result seems to be a nice kid who is just holding his own like a normal 15-year old would. There is even a 15-year old girl in school who seems to like him as a geek, not as a music star.

Anna is still living in Cottage #2 at the Farm. Her three-year old grandson, Zane, has been living with her the last six months. The baby was abandoned by his mother when he was three months old, and Anna's son tried to be a single dad for two years, but eventually it became too much for him. Zane is currently the youngest resident of the Farm. He is fun to watch on the bowling lanes – he still can't figure out why it is not okay to just walk down the lane and knock the pins down with your hands. Russ would agree with Zane – no rules needed…

Lynn is a frequent Farm visitor, mainly on the weekends when the grandchildren are often visiting as well. She is still involved in the grandchildren's lives. Dan lived with her in San Francisco for three months until he found an apartment of his own. Her Public Relations firm has continued to prosper, and it is a good focus for her time. She started dating again about a year ago, but if anything is serious yet, I do not know about it. Russ would be a tough act to follow.

Diana is a very special case --- we got married four years ago, one week after she got her graduate degree (And one year after I figured out 'where I was going' with my life – per Russ's instructions.)

Diana went to work for Facebook first. After a year there, Morgan Stanley made an offer that she decided to take. After two years of being an investment banker and working too many hours and traveling too often, she switched to one of the Sand Hill venture capital companies. It has worked out great… so far. *New mom*

And me… Russ's death dramatically changed what I was planning to do. Russ made me Executor of his will, but also a trustee for the trust he put the Farm into. The other trustees were his three children and Lynn. All the trustees can use the house for up to ten weeks a year.

The Farm trust was set up to pay Anna (or her replacement if she left) to keep the Farm the inviting place it had been.

Russ also made me the trustee of his investment trust, which provides financial assistance to his three children and eventually also the grandchildren. Initially, the investment trust employed Diana part-time to keep working with all the operating companies that she had been helping when Russ was alive.

A week after the July Fourth party, Matt Lawson offered me a full-time job at Fenwick & West. I said 'yes'. For the next three years I worked there.

Initially, after Russ died, I stayed in Cottage #6 at the Farm. I made a 'deal' with Matt Lawson that allowed me to work three days a week 'remotely' from the Farm. In this way I could combine my work managing the Farm with my work at Fenwick & West. I had grown to love living at the Farm.

After three months, Katlin, Mark, and Lynn suggested that I move into the main house. They said it made no sense to have me in the cottage and the master bedroom left empty. While all of Russ's personal stuff had been moved out a couple of months earlier, but it still felt very 'funny' to be sleeping in his room. It would always be his room in my mind.

Another reason for moving me into the main house was that everyone was all coming to the Farm frequently, almost as often as they did when Russ was alive. It had become a nice 'sanctuary'. They wanted to encourage me to stay, so that the house was still 'inviting' and had a 'lived in' feeling.

I found the plans Russ had for using some of the Farm to start an experimental organic farm near the stables. We were able to do that with UC-Berkeley in 2010. Students working on the organic farm live in a guest house in the stable area. In 2012, the local high schools started having field trips to the organic farm.

Helping Kevin with his music rights turned out to be the catalyst for my eventual career choice. At first, I just needed to learn the basics of the intellectual property laws around music. This effort was not much different than the intellectual property work I was doing at Fenwick & West.

Because of Kevin, however, I was starting to meet other people in the entertainment industry in San Francisco. I was soon giving casual advice to several of them. After a year, two of them wanted to hire me as their attorney. Because I was working at Fenwick & West, I couldn't do it.

I discussed the issue with Matt Lawson. He was able to change my status at Fenwick & West to 'of counsel', which meant I was independent and could do any outside legal work I wanted to take.

I expanded my small practice to include not only entertainment creators, but also independent software engineers. It has grown in the last three years and now I have two other lawyers working with me.

When I was first working at Fenwick & West, I rented a small studio apartment in Palo Alto to use a couple of nights a week. With Diana living in the graduate school housing on Stanford campus, we were only a mile apart.

She came to the Farm more often than anyone else because she was still doing part-time work for the investment trust and Russ's operating companies. So Cottage #1 was kept open for her, and she left clothes there to make it easier to go back and forth.

I am not sure 'how' or 'why' it happened, but I can tell you 'where' it happened... at the Far Veranda. Diana and I had taken a break one Saturday, and she suggested we walk up there for the wonderful view. One moment we were admiring the view and talking about how Russ loved it. The next moment, we were kissing...

Diana and I are expecting our first child, a boy, in two months... I think we will name him 'Russ'.

÷÷÷÷÷÷÷   ÷÷÷÷÷÷÷   ÷÷÷÷÷÷÷

The Happy Class Keys

Jay Knight

www.the-happy-class.com

Authors note: Most of these keys come from the book The Happy Class, but some of them and part of what is said about them are Russ Morrison's actual words taken from conversations that he and I had in 2008 that were not put in the book.

This summary is meant to be a quick reference guide to the Keys to Happiness that came from Russ Morrison.

Happiness: It is good to understand that there are two kinds of happiness. They are so similar it can be hard to tell them apart at times.

One, I call situational happiness. Like a first kiss with a new boy you like or heading down a steep rollercoaster or surfing a great wave or watching your child ride a bike with no training wheels for the first time. As you can imagine, the list of things that can cause situational happiness is nearly endless, so there is no shortage of opportunities.

The other one, I call True Happiness. Don't let my name confuse you. They are both important in your life. True Happiness is like waking up almost every morning excited about the day ahead even before you have thought about what kind of day it is likely to be. Sometimes it is said to be the people who have True Happiness see the 'glass half full rather than half empty'. But actually these people are happy when the glass is one quarter full, or an eighth full, or… I think you get it. These people are happy with who they are and the life they are living (given the circumstances they are living in, almost no matter what those circumstances are.)

So to maybe explain how these two forms of happiness work together, it might be like the ocean. Waves (like situational happiness) can come up high on shore and once they end, the water recedes back. But if you raise the whole water level/tide (True Happiness) then even the smaller waves come up higher on the shore.

One more note -- happiness is one of those emotional feelings that are hard to describe. Happiness feels different for different people who show it in different ways. But in the end, we all know what happiness is.

Practice can make you happier: You can actually improve your happiness level without changing your circumstances. It's like singing. I'm a terrible singer, but with some guidance and practice I would be less terrible. Happiness is like that. And while I have no interest in improving my singing ability, I am and maybe you are as well, usually interested in raising my happiness level no matter where it is. Improving your happiness will not come from reading a book, but from actually practicing what things in that book that work for you.

There are no rules, only respect for yourself and others: If you can keep this concept near the center of all you do, it makes being happy easier.

It's really two concepts pulled together. First is 'no rules'. If you had no rules, then there would be no expectations of others and thus no disappointments. No disappointments would mean a higher 'tide' of True Happiness. 'No rules' means to set others free to decide on their own what they will do. By not trying to control others, you save energy and disappointment for yourself, and others will respond with genuine interest in you, if they really do care about what you are proposing.

That said, humans are not too good with 'no rules'. They seem to need some guidance. One of my favorite movie lines is when the Kevin Spacey character in the movie *KPac*

;ked why there were no laws on his planet – his answer 'Every creature in God's universe knows the difference between right and wrong.' – Despite that humans seem to need more.

So I add the concept of respect, first for yourself and then for others. A simple example would be that out of respect for yourself you wouldn't give yourself drugs that destroy your brain and certainly out of respect of others, you wouldn't give those drugs to anyone else.

Another example could be keeping your room neat. You might make your bed every morning out of respect for yourself wanting see a nice bed when you get home in the evening. Out of respect for others, just closing the door to your room should be enough, so they do not have to see the mess.

This combination of no rules and respect goes a long way when being a parent. Before telling your child what to do, consider why you are doing it. Is it out of respect or just some old rule you thought was right....?

Death and God: This is probably the number one key to True Happiness.... the 'killer app'.

How do I make the best of the time I have .

All humans are mortal, and we all die. Actually, death is the defining characteristic of life. It's the one thing we all know will happen for sure.

Yet, it is a seldom discussed topic. It is even a seldom thought-about event. So my advice on this topic is to 'get over it', accept it, stop imagining that one day you will wake up and some scientist will have invented the live forever pill (we have all had that dream….)

For Atheists this is pretty straight forward, 'when it's over it's over'. So it's best to make the best of the only thing you know, your life.

For people believing in God (like me), no matter what their religious or non-religious beliefs are, it gets more complicated. But at some point, it comes down to 'do you feel lucky?' Or better put, 'Does God give humans any form of existence after death?'

To be happy, it makes little difference as to your beliefs, as the answer is pretty much the same. On this issue, you believe what you believe. And your belief has to get you past the point of worrying about dying. There is nothing you can do about it, as dying just happens…

You live the best life you can, and God is in control, you are not…

So, since you know that death is not worth worrying about, then nothing else can be so important that you need to worry about it. If you can stop worrying about the future, then you should be able to enjoy the True Happiness as it occurs in your life.

Decisions – 'the Box' and when to think: Making decisions can be one of the hardest things humans do. They fret, they worry, and they make themselves unhappy all during the process and even afterward by second guessing their decision.

I break decisions into two discussions – first is when to think. There are three types of decisions-- large important decisions, small repetitive decisions, and everything else. Big decisions are worth spending some time thinking about. Small repetitive decisions are worth figuring out a good answer to, like finding the quickest way to work and back since it happens a couple hundred times a year. All other decisions should not cause you much concern or thinking time. Just pick one choice quickly and move on.

This philosophy makes most decisions unthreatening, like which lane of the freeway to be in… Really, I have watched people get frustrated, put themselves and others in danger, just trying to get a better lane, which in and of itself often slows down around the next curve. And even if it doe. save two minutes, is the stress, high blood pressure, danger, etc. really worth it? Better to focus on the things that really matter.

The second item in decision-making is how to make big one-time decisions. I call my method of making these 'the box'. Just picture yourself in a box with high walls on all sides, but open at the top. The box is of course your current situation. Now figure out all the 'costs' of getting out of the box. And there are always 'costs', like having to give up friends, or job security, or the good things about your current location. Take your time thinking of the costs, and get them all in your mind. Make a list if there are too many to focus on at one time.

Then imagine yourself out of the box. What will it feel like, what will you be doing? No 'rose-colored glasses', just a realistic assessment.

Now compare the costs and what's it like being out of the box. Is there an obvious winner? If the winner is change, make the change. But just as important, is if the winner is no change. Then stop thinking about it. You have examined the choices and are making the right decision. Of course, later new facts may arise and create a different equation. Then you can do the process again.

People Do Not Change – at least not the way you want them to.

Missing this point can lead to spending time with, even marrying, the wrong people.

Try to avoid people who are trying to change you. You can feel this as they are often giving you 'gentle' hints on how you can be better at something.

Just as important, do not 'go after' someone who 'will be' perfect once you get them to change just a couple of things. It's best to assume that these people will not change the way you want. Then ask the question, 'if they do not change, do I want this person in my life?' – Just live with that answer or commit yourself to probably years of struggle with no satisfaction.

The Bell Curve: It looks a little like this . And most human behavior can be charted on a curve like it. For example IQ scores are like this with the most people, (the highest part of the curve) being at 100. The curve goes down as we increase (or decrease) the IQ score, so that at about 160 (or 40) we have a very low part of the curve (not many people). A bell curve like this one works to explain things like the ability to hit a baseball, dance to hip hop, etc.

The reason to understand this concept is that it often helps you understand what is going on. Is the big part of the curve right? Like the curve for how dangerous you think marijuana is... or gay marriage. Facts often do not cause the curve to move very quickly.

It is good to know where you are on the curve. Let's say singing, for example. Maybe if you are out on the singing curve where we had the 160 IQ people, maybe then you should spend more time on your singing ability. Conversely, if you are sitting on the middle of the curve, maybe it's best you enjoy other people's singing.

Again and again, you will see this curve as it applies to you and as it applies to the people around you and the world in general.

Relax – laugh: Many people are good at this one. If you have been finding yourself feeling tense, unhappy and under pressure, this is often a great little trick to use to defuse.

To relax, I personally use old movies. I can watch *You've Got Mail* at least once of month and still it relaxes me. Figure out what it is that will relax you, a competitive game of handball with your neighbor is not it, good exercise maybe, but you still need an escape.

Go find it…

Accept reality: Good news is usually easy to accept, so mainly I am talking about bad news here.

You got fired (or even just a warning), your boyfriend is moving out, or that sure fire investment just went to zero. You know the stuff I am talking about.

I do not mean skip the grieving time. Feeling sad about losing someone or something is part of healing. But the faster you accept your new reality, the faster you will make decisions and take actions that will work to bring happiness back to your life. Don't dwell on your loss. Dwell on what you are going to do now that you have suffered that loss.

Focusing on today rather than yesterday will bring more long-term happiness than spending too much time in the past.

Forgive, Forget, Move On - Don't Let Anyone/Anything Spoil Today or Tomorrow: This is pretty similar to Accept Reality. If you can forgive someone, that's great, if you can forget, that is good too. But even if you cannot forgive or forget, make sure that you 'move on'. That is the most important part.

The most important person to learn how to forgive is yourself. If you have made a mistake, get over it. You cannot go back and undo it. All you can do is learn how to forgive yourself so you can move forward.

You cannot stay happy being mad or frustrated at someone or something. Your boss skipped you over for a promotion and gave it to his cousin, or the guy who golfs with him on weekends or whatever. Maybe you cannot forgive or forget, but you can move on. And what does 'move on' look like? First accept reality. Your boss really did this thing. Now what do you do? Take your time. This sounds like a big decision, but there's no sense making a decision while you're emotional. Slow down and think about it. Stay or leave or???? After you have all your alternatives figured out, use the 'the box' and hopefully an obvious winner appears, and you can 'move on' (which may mean actually staying at that job... but probably not.)

Once you decide on how to 'move on' you'll start to feel better quickly – and you will be more receptive to the things that do make you happy.

Guilt/Mistakes: A great way to ruin today is feeling guilty about mistakes made in the past. I do not know how to say this any better. The past is over. You cannot change it, so once again accept reality and move on....

That said, the past definitely affects your present and your future, so ignoring the past is not a good plan either.

For example, you dumped your girlfriend for a new one. You realize too late that the old one really was much better for you. You wish you had never pushed her away... stop... stop wishing you had done things differently. You didn't, so accept reality, check your alternative and move on... even if 'move on' is a desperate attempt to see if she will take you back.

Of course, from her side, this is what it looks like. She made a mistake thinking you were a loyal trustworthy boyfriend. You broke her heart. She is wishing that either she had never met you or you were the kind of boyfriend she really wanted. If you make an attempt to try again, her decision becomes whether to not waste more time on you and get her heart broken all over again or give you a second chance... (My personal advice to her is 'people do not change', you will break her heart again, so 'move on' and let you go, but then who knows....)

Worry: This is the twin sister of Guilt. Simply put, worry is wasting today thinking about bad things that might happen in the future. Pointless. And worse, worry is a great killer of present happiness. Just stop.

This does not mean to throw all caution to the wind and just do whatever you want and the future be damned.

Planning for the future is a perfectly good use for part of today. And by definition, planning is thinking about the future. Buying life insurance, so your children have the money to go to college is planning for a bad event in the future… Living in a house that can withstand an earthquake is probably good planning in San Francisco, but maybe a waste of time in Racine, Wisconsin.

I think you get the difference. Thinking about bad things in the future (worrying) is a waste of time if there is no 'affordable' plan to solve the potential problem…

Who are you? What do you want your life to be about? And who will go with you? This is another of the important keys to True Happiness…

First make an honest assessment of yourself, things you do well, things you do poorly, things you like doing, things you do not like doing. Things like you really like meeting new people (or not). You love creative cooking, but not everyday cooking. You're good at math, and you are terrible at music. Write this stuff down and take your time doing it.

No wishful thinking here… and no judgments about yourself. If you are 30 pounds overweight… that doesn't mean you can't lose it, it just means right now you are 30 pounds overweight…

Next is what do you want your life to be about? This not a single answer question, as you can be a great mother, a good teacher, a local politician, a South American travel expert and an over 40 singles top ten tennis player in your city. Some of these can be 'big' goals and some can be smaller. And, yes, they will compete with each other for your time.

Now look at how you are spending your time in an average week and average month… Does it have any relationship to your skills? Does it have any relationship to the things you say you like to do? Are you giving your time to the things you say you want your life to be about. If not, why not?

Lastly, find someone who will be compatible with what you want your life to be about. If you do, those moments of happiness will increase… What if the woman described above (the mother, teacher, politician, traveler and tennis player) is dating a guy she met at the tennis club. He is not interested in politics, doesn't much like to travel, and has no children... I am not saying 'no' here, but remember, he is unlikely to change, so on those other important parts of your life you will probably be going it alone...

Will you change what you want your life to be about... probably 'yes'. I think the younger you are, the more often all these changes happen. There is nothing wrong with things changing. They may change for reasons you may not even be aware of. That said, when you change the direction of your life, it can cause major imbalances in the relationships you already have, especially with a spouse... I am not saying to fight changes to those things you know your spouse will not be joining you on, but do note that it can stress relationships and sometimes be the underlying cause of divorce later.

Believe in yourself, be your biggest cheerleader:
This is a hard one for some people. I am not telling you to start bragging to others about your skills or things you have done. The first thing is to believe in yourself, silently to yourself. Every human has things they are better at and worse at than other people.

I love music. I cannot sing a note nor keep a beat going with any instrument. But I did notice that I was good a picking what songs were going to be more popular than others. So whenever I heard a new song with friends, I would tell them what I thought… and I when I was right, I would remind them that I had picked that song. After a while, people started asking me what I thought of a new song… It felt good when they did…

Maybe you have read more about the Civil War than most people, maybe you know about Dilbert. If you cannot find a facet about yourself that you want to cheerlead, pick one out that you can learn. Believe in your ability to do that particular facet well and then focus on it.

Once you have one (or more) things you like about yourself, you will see life expand from there. Believing in yourself goes a long way toward having self-confidence and ultimately finding True Happiness.

One true friend: Let me make this one very easy. A good dog can be your one true friend. They have the advantage of always listening to you talk and always wanting to be with you no matter what. While dogs are great, it is great if you can find at least one person you can tell anything to with no fear. No fear of being told you are stupid. No fear of being told exactly what you should do. No fear of that friend betraying you. No fear of having that friend abandon you.

These true friends can be somewhat difficult to find. We often marry them. Sometimes we get these people early on in life. If you do, do not let them drift away. Technology makes distance not as much of a factor today. Call, chat, email, send photos.... stay in touch. You will need these friends more than once in your life. "In every life a little rain will fall" – and it will be much easier to get past it with one true friend.

Don't let your goals get in the way of your life: This often seems counter intuitive. If I am heading toward the things I want my life to be about, how can that be a problem?

One point to make here is to be sure that you are enjoying the process of obtaining any goal you have, and that even if you do not obtain that goal you will feel good about the time you spent on trying to get it...

A second point is that obtaining a goal may not come with the lasting excitement and happiness you might think. It is often true that the journey/process of reaching a goal brings more happiness than the final act of achievement.

A third point is to know what you're missing in the rest of your life while focusing on a goal or two.

It is a one, two, three punch against letting goals dominate your life. Do things that are not 'on point'. Take that trip to Europe before you are 30, even if you cannot 'afford' it. Travel real cheap; it can be done. Take road trips to parts of your country that you have not seen before. Go to the movies (not always waiting for them to show up on TV), go to a play, an opera, the ballet, an art museum, find a trail to walk on, join a gym with no hope of looking buff. Again the list is endless. Just experience life, before it's over.

One thing I sometimes do is to step back and pretend my life is a book that I am reading. I am the main character in my own book. The question I ask myself at those moments is, 'If I was reading this book, what would I want the main character to do next?' And the answer usually is not go back and work some more overtime or sit home another night watching mindless television.

Money: First, let me say that money is not the root of all evil. Let me also add that money cannot buy happiness (Oh, it can buy a few moments of situational happiness, but like a drug, you have to keep upping the stakes to make that work.)

I used to run a celebrity management company. If one of the bookkeepers was depressed over money, I would ask them, "As a group, who is happier, your clients or your friends?' The answer was nearly always 'They are pretty much the same'.

You need food, health, and safe shelter.

After that, money just buys different things in your life. Which is really more fun, trying to find the best taco place in Los Angeles or the best steak place in New York City? Actually, they both sound like fun to me….

One more thing to know -- Money can destroy happiness. More precisely the effort to get more money is what does the destroying. Don't spend or plan to spend more money than you have. It causes debt, especially credit card debt, the worse kind.

Credit card debt will eventually cause you to 'need' to work more to make more. If you want to work more because you are having so much fun at work, that is great. But working to make money to pay credit card debt means you have headed your life in the wrong direction. Happiness will not be found in credit card debt.

Do what you like doing as often as possible: If this seems like a 'duh' to you, that is good.

It's as simple as it sounds, except that many people can look and see just how few hours they spend each week actually doing what they really like doing. Do the math for the last month, and see how you stack up. It's up to you to decide what is the right amount of time spent on different things and what is the right balance…

Set them free: The 'them' are the people in your life -- your friends, your spouse, your children, your co-workers… everyone around you.

The freeing is your simply letting go of your expectations for them and letting them figure it all out for themselves.

Stop demanding that your daughter become a doctor or your husband make more money at his job. Or your children play soccer or go to the school dance.

You may have noticed that I offer more parent/child examples as in my experience that is the most important time when you need to set someone free.

When you give up your expectations for the people around you, you may be surprised at what decisions they do make, the achievements they accomplish. They will like you more for cheering them for what they want to do. And in the end, all of this will make you happier…

Don't forget to have fun: Fun comes in many ways. Lying next to a swimming pool doing nothing can be fun. Playing penny-ante poker with friends can be fun. Try seeing a good movie, reading a good book, playing Monopoly, going to a basketball game. There may be more ways to have fun than anything else. The trick is to do them -- Don't just 'plan' to do them, 'talk' about doing them, or 'wait' for the perfect moment to do them.

My personal plan is to try to do some kind of fun activity every day for at least an hour – but that is just me.

Giving and getting: Everyone does both in life. But givers seem to be happier than takers. They may have less 'stuff', but they are never worried that someone else has more than they do, and they are seldom short of people who want to be with them.

A second point here, not to be missed, is that, if possible, spend more of your time with givers than takers. It rubs off, and their spirit and happiness will help yours.

When I mean givers, I do not mean just material things, it's also time (like a friend helping you with your homework when there is nothing in it for that person), and support (like going to your band recital, or reading a poem you wrote).

Real givers never expect anything in return. Their reward is doing something they like to do, helping others.

If possible, be a giver....

Bonus thought...

Just say 'Yes': This is not really a happiness key. Maybe it's more like something that will give you a richer life.

The idea is simple. Just say 'yes' to things more often than you are comfortable saying that 'yes'. I do not mean to say 'yes' to things that are bad for you, like drugs or driving your car recklessly to show friends how cool you are.

I mean say 'yes' to things like – a trip to Africa, or the opera (for some people those are the same stretch). Try skiing (at least once), sing in your church choir even if you cannot sing (I did that one, it was fun, and I am sure I was never on the right note. But, the other members of the choir were happy that I tried... only once.)

I have met more interesting and special people and done more interesting things... simply by saying 'yes'. Try it.

÷:÷:÷:÷:÷

÷:÷:÷:÷:÷

The Happy Class books are available at Amazon or

www.the-happy-class.com

Follow us on Facebook at

www.facebook.com/TheHappyClass

Acknowledgements

I would like to give great thanks to Jessica Jorgensen and Katie Setterby for all their help, reviews, suggestions and encouragement. Without them, I would not have finished this. I would also like to thank my editor, Linda the WriteWatchman, for all her ideas and especially her patience with my poor typing, spelling and grammar skills.

About the author

The Happy Class is the second book by Jay Knight and first book is *Nothing Ventured*. Jay Knight is the 'pen name' of a business entrepreneur who lives in the Silicon Valley with his wife Lisa and their pug Q. *The Happy Class* is based on real life events witnessed by the author. The events and names have been altered to fit into one basic period of time.

Although the ideas are simple that's what makes them so applicable. I have found that when I do not use these tools, my life does not seem to go so well e.g. letting someone be free to allow them to choose